CW01513158

On Matters Human:
An Historian's Perspective

Nicholas Tarling

Edited by
Jeff Malpas *and* Rupert Wheeler

Exploring aspects of the human experience across time and place, this remarkable collection is a testimony to the breadth of Nicholas Tarling's knowledge of art, literature, music and world history. His stimulating treatment of topics that range from dignity and suffering to popular culture will appeal to all those who seek to understand the manifold expressions of the human condition.

Prof. Barbara Andaya, University of Hawai'i

Nicholas Tarling's erudition as a celebrated historian with particular interest in South East Asia is joined in these essays to wisdom deepened by his active involvement in the arts, theatre and music. His writing on these important subjects is also infused with the warmth and enthusiasm that characterised his oral presentations, making them a delight to read.

Dr. Ross Mellick. Neurologist, Sydney

What this collection of essays shows is how the history of Southeast was not merely the focus of Tarling's academic study, but was an intellectual lifeblood. In discussions of a wide range of topics, Tarling weaves his understanding of the region and its historiography into his analysis. Even the topic of opera, is seen through the eyes of a historian, and he asks us to understand cultural forms on their own terms and to see the common humanity. This then is the historian's perspective on human matters. Jeff Malpas and Rupert Wheeler have edited a collection of essays which bridge Tarling's wide-ranging interests to show us Tarling the humanist historian.

Associate Professor Nicki Tarulevicz, University of Tasmania

In his essays Nicholas shows us his remarkable breadth of scholarship. He uses his knowledge and love of music to illustrate its close links with some of the human emotions we strive to reflect in our musical performances.

Alexander Karpeyev D. Mus, Concert pianist

The essays in this book take us deep into the human mind, across societies and cultures, and through a broad sweep of history, reflecting on our human limitations and possibilities. From sparsely populated historical Southeast Asia to contemporary opera halls, they are at the same time a wonderful reflection of Nicholas Tarling's remarkable life and scholarship, in his own words.

Prof. Hugh Whittaker, Oxford University

Nicholas Tarling was a seemingly old-fashioned courtly gentleman but with an uncanny ability to not only comprehend but to be of our time, and totally modern. On reading his essays I can hear him speaking in his beautifully modulated voice - he makes words live. His great ability is to make the difficult comprehensible, the complex understandable and that shines through these short essays on very diverse topics.

Amanda Wojtowicz, ret. Academic & Director

Much more than a comprehensive overview of the many aspects of human experiences in the broad spectrum as suggested by the chapter titles, the refreshingly insightful angles used in many of the essays can only be given by someone with an unusual breadth of knowledge and cross-cultural training as Nicholas Tarling.

As a historian, he was uniquely equipped to share with readers concepts of miscellaneous human conditions in the most empathetic and humanitarian terms. Readers will find this Essay Collection a delightful and inspiring read.

Emeritus Professor Manying Ip, University of Auckland

Table of contents

Foreword i

1. On Dignity and Indignity.....................................1

2. On Suffering.. 13

3. On Hope.. 25

4. On Human Presence 37

5. On Human Complexity 55

6. On Judgment.. 71

7. On Opera.. 83

8. On Time and Place.. 87

9. On Popular Culture (in History and Theory)... 95

10. On Accounts and Explanations 121

Editorial Notes.. 133

Foreword

Nicholas Tarling is one of the foremost historians of the role of the British in Southeast Asia during the nineteenth and twentieth centuries. Well established in his field of expertise specifically focusing on British policy in and towards Malaya/Malaysia, Indonesia, Siam/Thailand and Myanmar (Burma), he has authored and edited close to 40 books including the two volume *The Cambridge History of Southeast Asia* (Cambridge, 1992), and more than 90 scholarly journal articles in an academic career spanning more than half a century. Nick, as he is affectionately known, is the quintessential scholar: a consummate researcher and a prolific writer. Poring through literally miles of archival documents is but second nature to him; likewise putting pen to paper for his findings, analysis, interpretations, thoughts and opinions to churn out manuscript after manuscript for publication. Apart from history, his forte, Nick wrote on higher education and on the performing arts (music and theatre).[1]

The forgoing accolade was penned in the late 2000s when I was guest editor of a themed volume, 'Themes for Thought on Southeast Asia: A Festschrift to Emeritus Professor Nicholas Tarling on the Occasion of His 75th Birthday' that appeared in *New Zealand Journal of Asian Studies*.[2] It was a collection of papers, duly revised, that were presented at the 'Southeast Asia: Past, Present and Future, International Conference in Honour of the 75th Birthday of Professor

---

[1] Ooi Keat Gin. Peter Nicholas Tarling: A Tribute. *International Journal of Asia Pacific Studies*, 13, 2 (2017): 161 [161-77]. First published in *New Zealand Journal of Asian Studies*, 11, 1 (2011): 15-30.

[2] Ooi Keat Gin (ed.), Themes for Thought on Southeast Asia: A Festschrift to Emeritus Professor Nicholas Tarling on the Occasion of His 75th Birthday, *New Zealand Journal of Asian Studies*, 11, 1 (June 2009): 1-446.

Nicholas Tarling' organized by the New Zealand Asia Institute, University of Auckland, on 1-3 February 2006. It was a gathering of renowned scholars of Southeast Asia, mainly historians, from across the globe who came to celebrate a highly respected scholar's milestone that of his 75th year.

On that occasion, I recalled vividly Nick's characteristic contemplative look as one speaker after another delivered their working papers. And in his incisive manner, he made some comments, expressed some sharp observations, the occasional critique or two, and his proffered suggestions for further consideration. A smile, rather it was a grin, when he cut the cake prior to our partaking dinner that evening. It was a celebration.

My last encounter with Nick was a decade later, on his 85th birthday in Manila which was planned to coincide with the 4th Nicholas Tarling Conference on Southeast Asian Studies on 1-2 February 2016. In between, there many get-togethers in various corners of his Southeast Asian 'playground', from Bangkok, Singapore to Hanoi, Kuala Lumpur.

Then, news of his passing was received via forwarded messages. The very first was when Professor Paul Clark e-mailed Emeritus Professors Anthony Reid and Wang Gungwu, on 17 May 2017, three days later.

> Please excuse the joint message, but I thought you should both know that Nick Tarling is no longer with us. Saturday afternoon (13 May) was a clear, late autumn, blue-sky, calm day and 20 degrees C here in Auckland. Nick went for a swim at the beach close by his home in Devonport. Someone noticed after ten minutes that he was not moving. Medical people, who happened to be at a gathering at the beachside boat club, tried their best to revive him, but, without success.

Then, Clark wrote me on the 26th. 'We all expected to have Nick with us for at least another ten years.'

Bangkok was to be our next meet-up, but political instability disrupted our plans. Then, his demise.

Nick may have gone, but memories of him remained, etched in our minds and hearts, recollections from direct personal encounters, or indirectly through his writings, in speaking to us from history tomes to musical and operatic reviews. Moreover, he left us with more than 60 book-length works which could easily filled several book shelves, not to mention his hundred over articles in scholarly journals besides his enormous music collection of vinyl records, CDs, etc., and his personal papers, notes, drafts, documents … running into thousands of pages.

One of the last of Nick's books, if I remembered correctly (he occasionally multi-tasked several writing projects in tandem), described as an "unusual book" was *Recalling Childhood*,[3] an edited volume that was published posthumously. I recalled of us discussing (mainly through e-mails) the genesis of the idea and its conceptual format and contents, criterion of childhood, and task of enticing contributors. We were supposed to be co-editors. But then I had too much, more than I can possibly chew piled on my table. None perturbed, the indefatigable Nick, then in his nid-80s, undertook most of the groundwork and follow-ups with contributors. I regretted in not being *more helpful* to him then.

The present volume, *On Matters Human: An Historian's Perspective* is an insightful offering allowing us to have glimpses of the illuminating philosophical thoughts and mind of Nicholas Tarling. In nine pieces, he expresses and shares his thoughts, opinions, viewpoints, interpretations on a series of matters concerning us as humans. Themes ranged from dignity and indignity, suffering, human presence to judgement, time and place, popular culture. Delightfully interesting, but at the same time, intriguing, even perplexing, we gather through this volume gaining much insightful knowledge, from the benefits of a keen eye on human behaviour and misbehaviour, thoughts drawn from

---

[3] Nicholas Tarling (ed), *Recalling Childhood*. With the assistance of Ooi Keat Gin and Rupert Wheeler (Lanham, MD: Hamilton Books, 2017).

contemplations and recollections, and wisdom borne through age.

Although penned by a professional historian, the philosophical thoughts and commentaries draw anecdotes and illustrations drawn from the world of music, literature, and others, besides history. In 'On Human Presence' (chapter 4), he draws analogies mined from various fields and disciplines to illustrate 'non-presence' of humans, such as, of Southeast Asia in the past,

> [of] the demographic immaturity of the region [Southeast Asia]. Thinly populated till recent times, maybe only 30m in 1830, but now perhaps 600m, but there are still areas of empty jungle. You might there see or hear no human, though other wildlife might be present.

In comparison to a musical analogy,

> Some find the non-presence of human beings a comfort, an excitement. They have climbed the top of the mountain as in Strauss's *Alpine Symphony* and are exhilarated by the prospect and also by their own achievement, though rarely done all on their own, any more than that of a Trans-Tasman swimmer.

But, he reminds us,

> Others find it unbearable, particularly if they have lost a long-term companion. They may seek to communicate with them, or even imagine that they see them.

On the other hand, drawing from real life experiences,

> Some have seclusion thrust upon them – [in] prison, solitary confinement – and the object [of the jailers] is to break their [prisoners'] spirit. [And] Terry Waite [hostage in Lebanon] was not even allowed a book'.

Or drawn from literature,

Marooned on Juan Fernandez in 1704, Alexander Selkirk's life was not, it seems, as Daniel Defoe was to depict in *Robinson Crusoe*. He was brutalised. When found in 1709 he had more or less lost the power of speech, having 'so much forgot his Language for want of Use, we could scarce understand him'.

Always the historian, Nick, again and again, in helping us, the readers, to comprehend, to grasp a certain phenomenon, an emotion, turned to tales from the past to enlighten our thoughts and further our understanding. In commenting on 'Dignity and Indignity' (chapter 1) which are associated with the concept of human 'worth', traditional Southeast Asian society are brought to illustrate and compare, namely of slaves and bondsmen. He cited the action of the father of Hang Tuah, the foremost folk-hero of the Malays, in presenting himself to the *Datuk Bendahara*, the vizier, as a *hamba* to him. The term *hamba* commonly 'used to cover what in the West would be covered by a range of words, subject, vassal or slave', but in the Malay world, 'The focus was … not on the degree of legal freedom a person might possess, but on the object of a person's obligation, and thus of his or her niche in society', likewise, applicable similar terms such as '*kyun* in Pagan Burma, *phrai* in Siam … *ata* in the Bugis world'.

Enlivening the prose as well as enriching and widening our knowledge from the world of history, literature, opera, music, *On Matters Human* makes us be more conscious of ourselves as human beings, as ourselves, living on our own, with others, interrelating to one another, and much more.

Ooi Keat Gin
The Pongo
November 2020

1. On Dignity and Indignity

The meaning of words slip and slide, though rarely perhaps entirely perishing. Is that true particularly of words that describe and generalize about human relationships? Those change restlessly or are changed, in part indeed by the application of words to them. Think for example of 'ethnic', 'gay', 'community', of 'human resources', 'accountability', 'excellence' and 'peer review', of 'mission' and 'services', words with suspiciously military overtones.

Among those the word 'dignity' must be included. Throughout its linguistic life — and some words can be virtually murdered by usage and misusage, though they may retain a capacity to haunt or spook or, ignis fatuus, lead astray — it has retained an association with the concept of human 'worth'. Like other words that seek to describe or determine human relationships, it is not an absolute matter, even at a particular period, but one that relates an individual to other individuals or to a larger 'society' or 'community'. Even a concept of 'self-worth' appears to depend on a relationship with others. Our own estimate of ourselves is surely always comparative: I measure up to, or am better than, others; or I fulfill, or exceed, the norms they have set. They are mistaken about me: there may be an element of assertion, even defiance, or of despair.

'Dignity' was not always associated with equality, as it is now in the language of rights. 'All human beings are born free and equal in dignity and rights. They are endowed with reason and conscience and should act towards one another in a spirit of brotherhood.'[1] That spirit was presumably not that of Cain and Abel, but rather one designed to challenge patriarchy or hierarchy. It is a political or ideological statement: the second sentence offers a programme for realizing the principle of the first.

Even a cursory perusal of earlier meanings, however, suggests rather that dignity was associated with hierarchy. It was a noun that described the position of the planets in the

---

[1] *Universal Declaration of Human Rights* (1948), Art. 1.

heavens, and of men (and a few women) of high estate on earth: the 'worthies', though that had or came to have a slightly contemptuous or mocking connotation; the 'quality' in an earlier meaning differentiated from our notions of 'assessment' or 'fitness for purpose'. It was a matter of rank and honour, of title and office, and, of course, among the various disciplines that engaged the human brain was the 'dignity of philosophical enquiry', no doubt, at least in some cases, marked by 'excellence'.

Indignity, by contrast, covered not only 'unworthiness' — in the sense of our own behaviour — but, more commonly, unworthiness of treatment, slight, administered to us by others. That, too, was related to hierarchy or breach of hierarchy, though it could later apply more or less to worth in the broader sense implied by the UN declaration. The same goes for 'indignation', anger at what is regarded as unworthy.

The shift in meanings seems crucial. Ours relates to a perception of humanity deeply affected by the Enlightenment, the revolutionary thinking of the American and French revolutions, and the Romantic emphasis on the individual. Dignity or indignity is associated with our person — physically, emotionally, mentally — rather than our social standing. We are, or ought to be, 'free and equal in dignity and rights'.

But we cannot assume that what is now is what has been nor that what is true of some is true of all: Japanese prisoners-of-war suffered less 'indignity' than Iraqis have more recently in being stripped, since nakedness was not abhorrent to them. Historians, whatever the 'dignity' of their enquiry, do face a dilemma that is also a challenge, answering which will never be complete but may be productive. We can enquire into the past with our own concerns in mind: perhaps we can do nothing else, however much we attempt objectivity. But we have to do it without assuming that its concerns were necessarily ours: otherwise all claim to objectivity has to be abandoned. The historian must read, but not read into or read back. Historiographical practice is meant to control subjectivity, though it cannot eliminate it. Recognition of that, on the other hand, need not amount to total relativism. If there is a judgment to be made, it should be seen as such.

Things are different, but that does not make them equally 'acceptable', 'valid' or 'appropriate', to use our debased currency of praise and blame.

How far can we thus assume that what we see as 'dignity' or 'indignity' had in earlier ages or has in other societies the same parameters or overtones as it has in our usage? It might be, for example, that in a hierarchical society, it was not only the 'quality' that were worthy. Others would, like Ishiguro's butler, find 'dignity' in a recognised place in the hierarchy, rather than positing an 'equality', and suffer indignity, not because of that, but because it was denied or not recognised. In 'service' at Hatfield House in the 1930s, Flo Wadlow was recently asked on TV whether she was happy with the system. 'I felt proud and privileged', she declared. 'I felt elevated as well.'[2] Allow that 'Flo', as she was called, remembered, as most of us, the sunny days rather than the stormy. But infer that hierarchy gave you not only a wage but a 'place'. Retainers shared in a measure the 'dignity' of their masters. Such positioning might limit rather than enhance arbitrariness. Indeed, it imposed some obligation on the masters, the lords, squires, patrons, who might help an able child with a scholarship, or keep a servant on well after he or she could effectively serve. The price of equality might, by contrast, be an insecurity that could lead to 'indignity'.

The Universal Declaration of Human Rights [Art. 4] also, of course, condemns slavery. How far the possible advantages of hierarchy might apply to slaves perhaps depends on the nature of the slavery involved. It is hard not to see 'chattel' slavery as an indignity, though we must be less sure that it was seen, let alone described, by those who suffered it as an 'indignity'. At least in respect of some of its forms in Southeast Asia, my own area of expertise, it was seen as an advantage. 'Slavery', like 'piracy', is indeed a term laden with Western associations that make it hard to use in Southeast Asian history. The main contrast seems to lie in the continuity between slavery and other forms of dependency, sustained in Southeast Asia but not in the West. That tended, too, to muffle the concept of 'freedom', even if in the West itself

---

[2] BBC Radio 4, 14 August, 2004.

'freedom' did and does not imply a total lack of obligation. The words in current use in general do not relate to a distinction between slave and free. Only *merdeka* took on that character in an earlier period. That itself derived, however, from a term used in Sri Vijaya to describe a chief or leader of a group of subjects or bondmen, in turn derived from a Sanskrit description of a person of great spiritual power or wealth.[3]

Traditional Southeast Asia

The control of men, rather than of land, was the key to the social systems of traditional Southeast Asia, sparsely populated for most of its history: they were, as Europeans used to say, worth their weight in gold. 'The Raja looks to the number of his following as the gauge of his power', wrote Frank Swettenham in Malaya in 1875, 'and other Rajas will respect and fear him accordingly. Thus, he tries to get men into his service.'[4] What was important to leaders and would-be leaders was the men and women whom they could place in a dependent relationship. 'For the poor and weak, on the other hand, security and opportunity depended upon being bonded to someone strong enough to look after them.'[5] The father of Hang Tuah, the folk-hero of the Malays, 'went in search of a living, and, presenting himself to the *Datuk Bendahara*, he made himself *hamba* to him'.[6] The focus was therefore not on the degree of legal freedom a person might possess, but on the object of a person's obligation, and thus of his or her niche in society. The same terms — *kyun* in Pagan Burma, *phrai* in Siam, *hamba* in the Malay world, *ata* in the

---

[3] Anthony Reid,(ed.), *Slavery, Bondage and Dependency in Southeast Asia* (St Lucia: University of Queensland Press, 1983), p.21.

[4] J. M. Gullick, *Indigenous Political Systems of Western Malaya* (London: Athlone, 1958), p.98.

[5] Reid, (ed.), *Slavery, Bondage and Dependency in Southeast Asia*, p.8.

[6] Quoted in Patrick Sullivan, *Social Relations of Dependence in a Malay State: Nineteenth Century Perak* (Kuala Lumpur: MBRAS, 1982), p.63.

Bugis world, were used to cover what in the West would be covered by a range of words, subject, vassal or slave.

These bonds were transferable, 'and it is this', Anthony Reid suggests, 'that provides the overlap with slavery'. Bondsmen could be 'presented as a marriage gift, donated to a monastery, offered as tribute, given as security for a loan, sold or inherited'. Yet the imagery throughout was 'that of the extended family', and even a slave was 'permitted a level of intimacy with his master which no one who was not a member of the household could dare assume'.[7]

The origin of this system of obligation commonly lay in debt. Meeting ritual obligation was one source of debt, gambling another. 'Sale or commendation of oneself and/or one's wife and children to a wealthier person' was a way out of 'severe hardship'. 'Pawning one's dependants or oneself..., or else entering a very unequal partnership with the creditor who became the patron if not the master, were the common Southeast Asian means of obtaining capital.'[8] Theoretically the debt could be redeemed, and that was to enable Europeans to draw a distinction between 'debt' slavery and what they regarded as 'true' slavery. In fact, labour was not sufficient to redeem the capital, but only to pay the interest. Of the pre-Spanish Filipinos Antonio de Morga wrote: 'it is to be understood that they made these slaves during their wars and differences: and most frequently on account of loans and usurious contracts, which were current among them, the payment, stock and debt increasing with delay, until they remained as slaves.'[9] The relationship was not seen in terms of cash return. The term for debtor in nineteenth-century Perak, for example, was *kawan* or companion, and in Sumatra *pengiring* or follower. 'Nor has the debtor under this system any

---

[7] Reid, *Slavery, Bondage and Dependency in Southeast Asia*, pp.8-9.
[8] Ibid., p.9-11.
[9] Hon. H. E. J Stanley, *The Philippine Islands, Moluccas, Siam, Cambodia, Japan and China at the close of the sixteenth century, by Antonio De Morga. Translated from the Spanish, with notes and a preface, and a letter from Luis Vaez de Torres describing his voyage through the Torres straits*, Hakluyt Society, First Series, 39 (London: Hakluyt Society, 1868), pp.299-300.

means of becoming free, unless some relative or friend comes forward to pay for him; and even in this case the creditor might if he so willed, and if were a Rajah in all probability would, under some pretext, refuse the offer of payment.'[10]

That does not, however, mean that these were slave societies, Reid insists, 'since the legal categories of slave and free were not well defined, obligation and fealty were more central to the Southeast Asian system than status-as-property, while in certain cases serf seems a more appropriate word than slave'.[11] Even this W. H. Scott doubted. The Visayan *oripun* and the Tagalog *alipin* were not slaves but, being bound not to the soil but to other men, they were not serfs either.[12] Nor, Reid himself adds, did the distinction between 'savage' slaves, captured or bought from the hill people, persist after in its initial harshness.[13] The same seems to be true of sea captives. 'A master was liable to neglect a *bangaya* who was remiss in his duties, but their statements and travel accounts of observers reveal that slaves, especially those with knowledge and skills, had good relations with their master and were not easily distinguished among their following.'[14] Harshness certainly existed, but it could be counter-productive. Labour was scarce, and the state administrations were rarely strong enough to enforce a bond challenged by a pull factor as well as a push factor. Debt bondage was indeed preferred to state service in Taung-ngu Burma.

Unable to acquire labour for their new urban centres because the free market was limited, and because they lacked the traditional ties that substituted for it, the early Europeans in Southeast Asia resorted to recruiting slaves, preferably from remote areas, India, Madagascar, Arakan, or New Guinea. They fell into Southeast Asian ways, however. The tyranny in Batavia, the Dutch Company's capital, was of the

---

[10] Quoted in Sullivan, *Social Relations of Dependence in a Malay State: Nineteenth Century Perak,* p.50.

[11] Reid, *Slavery, Bondage and Dependency in Southeast Asia,* p.12.

[12] Ibid., p.153.

[13] Ibid., p.12.

[14] James F. Warren, *The Sulu Zone* (Singapore: Singapore UP, 1981), p.219.

domestic sort. Slaves might be badly treated, but that was true of the lower orders more generally. 'The master has all power over the Slave, except that of killing him', La Loubere wrote of late seventeenth century Siam; 'And tho' some may report, that Slaves are severely beaten there (which is very probable in a country where free persons are so rigidly *bastinado'd*) yet the slavery there is so gentle, or, if you will, the Liberty is so abject, that it is become a Proverb, that the Siamese sell it to eat of a. Durion'.[15]

Modern states

While there could be an undue rush of sentiment for the slave-owning Old South, neglecting the violence intermingled with or implicit in or part of the patriarchy, was it better, or felt to be better, to be a 'wage-slave' in an atomised industrializing modernising and urbanising society subject to other forms of violence and degradation? One is reminded, though not quite relevantly, of the redoubtable Tory MP Cal. Sibthorp, who intervened in the debate in which Richard Cobden and John Bright questioned James Brooke's attacks on Dayak 'pirates' in the Borneo of the 1840s. 'There was cruelty enough practised by the free traders at home to those unfortunate persons who were in their employ, and they should begin by putting a stop to that.'[16]

The great economic changes of the nineteenth and twentieth centuries were indeed accompanied by a destruction of old hierarchies and a construction of new forms of association, based on 'nation', race or ethnic, religious affiliation, and employee union, in which individuals sought to find a place, to understand the world, to attain security. In all these changes, it seems clear, there was an increasing sense of individual worth and a shifting view of dignity. But they were coupled with a readiness to submit, if not to new hierarchies, to new obligations in states, societies and communities, in unions and churches, as the price of that

---

[15] Quoted in Reid, *Slavery, Bondage and Dependency in Southeast Asia*, p.24.

[16] *Hansard*, cxi, col. 301.

security, that recognition of human worth which older hierarchies may once have offered. To that the spread of literacy contributed. The risk was that you would lose your autonomy as the price of belonging, have to strike, avoid consuming certain foods or drinks, cover the face, vote as the party said. Those might be indignities, though some seemed and seem positively to enjoy them, finding security in compliance and identity in conformity. If you sought to preserve personal privacy, respect for which Peregrine Worsthorne may not be alone in seeing as contemporarily a prerequisite for dignity, you might only provoke our prurience, stimulate our voyeurism.

The state itself played an ambivalent role. Seeking efficiency, it became more active, made itself better informed about citizens or subjects, indeed defined who qualified or was to be disqualified on the basis of various criteria, residence, 'ethnicity', religion, changed their status and sought to tax them more effectively. At the same time as it grew stronger and brought itself into closer contact with the individual, it offered, often reluctantly but necessarily, greater participation. In that way the state increased its power and capacity to mobilise resources, human and otherwise, beyond anything achieved by the most authoritarian regimes in earlier ages. In counterpoint the discourse of 'rights' was extended in scope and more widely used. And as a world of states was created, that ambivalence was extended. Setting out rights in UN documents was coupled with the full acceptance of state sovereignty. The state was and remains both a potential protector and a potential violator.

The role of the state is ambiguous in another sense. The creation of a world of states may be seen as one kind of 'globalisation'. More commonly, it is a word we apply to the changes in the economic and cultural fields and in communications that, present at least since the industrialisation of the nineteenth century, appear to have gathered speed and increased scope from the late twentieth, though we must also interpret the word as a programme or ideology rather than a description. We could perhaps re-employ Sibthorp's comments on the free traders. Here is another process that destroys old hierarchies and obligations or changes their nature, and one not contained by any formal framework of responsibility or 'accountability' other than a financial bottom line. The state often promotes the process, but it also constrains it. It is the main, though not the only, means by which the impact of economic forces is mediated and either intensified or moderated. Will it prevent our finding other sources of security, and dignity, in association or in isolation, or will it encourage it? Will it act like on old-fashioned patron? Or will it act like the rent-oriented and disobliging landlord that replaced him?

The trends are at best dual, suggesting again that equality and dignity are not necessarily or readily associated. Continental human rights jurisprudence, it has recently been argued, has been and is being shaped by the concept of the right to an honourable image. Fascism diffused traditional marks of dignity to all members of the Volk and passed new laws against insulting ordinary people. Now that notion has extended to all citizens: 'an old aristocratic priority...has travelled into the present via Fascist law.'[17] Contrast the corporate world in its dealings with customers. We are given numbers, like soldiers, and our 'loyalty' is reduced to continued shopping. We are also at risk of losing our identity and thus our dignity. First names are used as in nursing homes and, I believe, brothels. Am I alone in seeing this as spuriously friendly but actually demeaning? We lose not only our good name, but any name: ignominy indeed. Dropping surnames, as Penelope Lively puts it in one of her novels, suggests not intimacy but a kind of indifference.[18]

Colonial states

Colonial states were even more ambivalent than their Western contemporaries. Imperialism involved an extension to them of the modernisation to which their masters were subjecting themselves, but it was necessarily even more incomplete. Once established, their administrations required revenue: they

---

[17] D. Gordon, *Times Literary Supplement*, 13 August, 2004, summarizing James, quoted in Whitman.

[18] Penelope Lively, *Perfect Happiness* (London: Heinemann, 1983), p.105.

had to create the conditions for and encourage investment, to build up infrastructure, to offer a measure of literacy. But how far could they go without undermining the colonial state? Industrialising was likely to be at odds with metropolitan interests. Extending political participation would lose control, offering at best only a limited extension of tenure to the colonial power. Independence was the only possible basis for a fuller modernisation. Securing that became the objective of 'nationalist' movements.

The historian can feel more certain than in respect of earlier hierarchies of the role of `dignity' in respect of the formation and expansion of such movements. It seems clear that we would resent the 'indignities' of the colonial state and of colonial or pseudo-colonial society, especially, but not exclusively, where there were colonies and where 'unacceptable' hierarchies were imposed. We can also be clear that, whether hierarchies were previously acceptable before or not, now they were definitely not, neither the old ones, often turned to account by imperial regimes, nor the new, since they were criticised in language with which we are familiar, the language, indeed, of the imperialists themselves. Much of the education the Spaniards offered in the Philippines was in the liberal arts, law, theology, and medicine. 'Was it at all surprising that education of this sort should produce Filipinos who thought they knew the rights of citizens and the duties of government...and who had the impudence to invoke Rousseau and the Laws of the Indies?'[19]

Everyday slights may have been more demeaning than the lack of political participation, though the ambition came to be independence. Certainly, that was the basis of the critique the second Raja of Sarawak, Charles Brooke, offered of imperialism in a pamphlet published in 1907 as part of a campaign against British interposition in Brunei. British possessions, he thought, were too much Anglicised. Good and friendly feeling had, he believed, existed in the early part of the nineteenth century. There had been a falling-off, a

---

[19] Quoted in R. A. Oades, *The social and economic background of Philippine nationalism*, PhD thesis, University of Hawaii, 1972, pp.269-270.

separation 'in consequence of the English developing into a higher civilization, as it is termed, among themselves with wives and families, and European luxuries, and so it has happened that though we govern, we only do so by power, and not by friendly intercourse or feeling'. Countries without colonial possessions faced a happier future than those with them. 'My own opinion is that before we reach the middle of this century all nations now holding large colonial possessions will have met with very severe reverses.'[20]

The forecast was accurate, though what happened did not happen in the way he expected. But if we accept that the downfall of empire was in some part at least the result of the arrogance the Raja criticised, again we may be talking of an elite: how far were these 'indignities' perceived as such not by the 'quality' but by the mass of the people? who might be used to, or not be aware of, foreign rule? who were yet to be uprooted by economic and governmental change? who might be badly treated by their own elites, the newer among whom might indeed be less sensitive to traditional obligations than the old? When they were recruited into nationalist movements, it was often indeed on other more oblique and traditionalist grounds.

China did not, of course, come under control by the Western 'imperialists'. Instead it compromised. The 'unequal' treaties it made in the nineteenth century came to be seen by later generations as 'national humiliations'. At the time, they were seen differently, and at least before the conflict with Japan of 1894-5, the Qing empire was dealing quite successfully with the challenges with which 'imperialism' presented it.[21] The language of 'national humiliation' took hold, however, on the often anti-Manchu intelligentsia and boosted their 'anti-imperialist' nationalism. How far the masses shared it is, however, surely questionable.

---

[20] Charles Brooke, *Queries: Past. Present and Future* (London: The Planet Offices, 1907), pp.13-14.

[21] Cf. S.A.M. Adshead, *The End of the Chinese Empire*, (Auckland: Heinemann, 1973), p.11-12.

The same perhaps applies in respect of nationalist movements developed in face of imperial rule. Indeed, the question goes deeper. In the Philippines, the great politico Manuel Quezon declared that he would prefer a government 'run like hell by Filipinos to one run like heaven by Americans'[22] Destroying 'national humiliation' surely guaranteed nothing to the masses.

The process is indeed in some cases replicated. The people of West Papua, consigned to Indonesian rule in the 1960s, see themselves as treated like animals, those with jobs kept in low positions. 'Educated Papuans regard common Indonesian attitudes towards themselves and other Papuans as personal insults, in much the same way as pre-war Indonesian nationalists responded to Dutch prejudices.'[23]

Writing on the rise and fall of British India, Karl de Schweinitz pre-figured Edward Said. 'If the coercive burden of the old imperialism has become internalized in, and diffused among, many states, who can say that it has become lighter?...One must hope that in the struggle for equity and justice, the world's states do not in their name impose more appalling restrictions on individuals and groups than did the nineteenth-century imperialists in the maintenance of their rule.'[24] The hope often seems a vain one. But I would not argue, like Michael Hardt and Antonio Negri, that the state is vanishing and ought to vanish.[25] Both in action and restraint

---

[22] Quoted in A. Gopinath, *Manuel L. Quezon: the tutelary democrat* (Quezon City, Philippines: New Day Publishers, 1987), p.12.

[23] R. Chauvel, 'Papua and Indonesia: where contending nationalisms meet', in D. Kingsbury, and H. Aveling, (eds.), *Autonomy and Disintegration in Indonesia* (London: Routledge Curzon, 2003), pp.120-121.

[24] Karl de Schweinitz., *The Rise and Fall of British India* (London: Methuen, 1983), p.256.

[25] M. Hardt and A. Negri., *Empire* (Cambridge, Mass.: Harvard University Press, 2000), p.336.

it is at least potentially and often actually the best guarantee that we have that the mass of people can live in 'dignity'.

Dignity Today?

We have created a world globalised in the sense that it is partitioned among sovereign states and globalising in the sense that economic and social trends are being powerfully spurred by electronic media. It is one that talks of privacy in the very process of destroying any chance of it. It perversely creates anonymity by the use of first names and promotes the commodification of people in the practice of 'management'. While it speaks the language of choice, most people on earth have the most limited of options. Their dignity and their rights are endorsed but not effectuated.

The hierarchical societies of the past encompassed oppression, even enslavement. In many cases, however, obligation was mutual, and dignity was not found merely in stoic acceptance of 'fate'. Displacing hierarchy by liberty and equality was to be accompanied by fraternity. At the very least, our societies must recapture a sense of mutuality, and create conditions under which people can find a measure of identity, security and dignity without resort to damaging others.

This chapter first appeared in Perspectives on Human Dignity: A Conversation, *edited Jeff Malpas and Norelle Lickiss (Dordrecht: Springer, 2007).*

2. On Suffering

You will expect an historian to think and speak in terms of time, and of what Adrian Moulyn calls 'objective' time, time that is measured by clocks and calendars, rather than 'subjective' time, time that is less mathematically measured by an individual's memory and recalled experience.[1]

In the course of time – both kinds, but particularly the former – the historian will point out, with the aid of the lexicographer, that the meanings of words change: they 'slip, slide, perish,' as Eliot put it, but are also revised or reappropriated. The verb 'suffer' has two main meanings. One relates to the undergoing of generally painful experience. 'A brave man suffers in silence.' 'He had suffered from delirium tremens.' The other relates to allowing or tolerating. 'I was not suffered to stir far from the house, lest I should run away.' 'Suffer the little children to come unto Me.' The second meaning has largely perished. Perhaps it retains a foothold in an adjectival opposite, 'insufferable,' though even that useful word has been displaced, like 'wrong,' by the pussyfooting 'inappropriate.'

Yet the two meanings may have had a connexion, and that may introduce a discussion, not of the meaning of the word 'suffering,' but of the 'meaning,' if any, of the experience. The connexion surely implies that the experience was something to be borne, to be endured, put up with. 'Suffering' as a noun was indeed defined as patient endurance, long-suffering, and as an adjective it suggested 'inured to suffering,' 'submissive.'

Perhaps these shifts point to changes over time in the conception of the experience, in the ways it is given 'meaning.' That raises fundamental questions to which all our disciplines offer but a partial answer, and history, perhaps, not one of the larger. They relate to the mysteries of the human condition itself. 'Suffering' relates to a whole range of experiences and it is both general and individual. What some experience as a major form of suffering, others find quite minor. Some cope

---

[1] Adrian C. Moulyn, *The Meaning of Suffering* (Westport: Greenwood Press, 1982), p.15.

better than others with what are among its major sources: the dread of death, the fear of loneliness.

In the past religions offered meanings now less readily acceptable. They also offered the prospect of redemption. For the Buddhists suffering was a fundamental constituent of being, a punishment for sins committed in a previous incarnation. To supersede the suffering that arose from desire, one must leave desire behind, leave the world behind. For the people of Israel, suffering was the punishment of sins committed by individuals and by the whole community. A messiah would bring redemption. In Christianity, suffering comes from sin. But God loves the world and gives his Son as a promise of redemption to those who are penitent and love Him.

These ideas remained and remain potent. They were, of course, challenged, by both the Enlightenment and by Romanticism. What alternatives did they offer? For the Romantic artist, the answer might be an 'heroic' approach. Through a work of your own creation, you would both use and displace suffering, investing in a hedge against annihilation.

It was not necessarily, however, entirely a matter of finding alternatives. In the grip of his own suffering – torn between spiritual aspiration and fleshly pleasure – Wagner focused his creative work on the theme of 'redemption.' In Parsifal, the Redeemer himself is redeemed, since his sacrifice is shown not to be in vain. 'The intended outcome of Christ's voluntary deed of suffering is fulfilled through imitation.' Parsifal is the redeemer of the Redeemer. He imitates Christ and 'completes Christ's deed of salvation through this imitation.'[2]

Wagner's sufferings were not material. Though at times in poverty or in flight, he was seldom at a loss for support or patronage, however outrageous his behaviour. When the outlook was bleak, he called, rightly perhaps, for champagne.

---

[2] Ulrike Kienzle, 'Parsifal and religion: a Christian music drama?' in A Companion to Wagner's Parsifal, ed. W. Kinderman and Katherine R. Syer (Rochester, Woodbridge: Camden House, 2005), pp.128-9.

Yet for many Romantics material suffering was essential for the production of 'great' art.

Certainly, that was the background for the 'Bohemia' of the Paris of Louis Philippe, so brilliantly depicted by Henri Murger, and later, by a process just short of sentimentalization, made into the most popular of operas by Puccini. It was inhabited by men like the Desbrosses brothers, one nicknamed 'The Christ,' one 'The Gothic.' They spent 'half the day not eating and the other half of dying of cold.... As for a fire, all they have is their pipes – very often without tobacco.'[3] It was also inhabited by 'amateurs.' 'To enter that paradise they leave their home, or the study which would have brought about a sure result, turning their backs abruptly on an honourable career for the quest of adventures and a life of uncertain chances. But since the most robust can hardly cling to a mode of life which would send Hercules into a consumption, they throw up the game before long, scamper back in hot haste to the paternal roast, marry their little cousin, set up as notaries in some town of thirty thousand inhabitants, and of an evening by the fireside they have the satisfaction of telling 'what they went through in their artist days,' with all the pride of a traveller's tale of his tiger hunt.'[4]

The legend of the artist in his garret had been born. If it did not exist, suffering had to be invented if 'art' were to be created. 'If you are really to develop to your full stature,' W.H. Auden told Benjamin Britten in 1942, 'you will have, I think, to suffer, and make others suffer in ways which are totally strange to you at present.'[5]

The notion that there is a connexion has endured, and there may be a truth in it. Shostakovich, Richard Taruskin has suggested, 'was perhaps the most pestered composer who

---

[3] Joanna Richardson, 'Henry Murger and 'La vie de bohème,'' in *English National Opera Guide*, no.14 (London: Calder, 1982), p.36.

[4] H. Murger, Preface to *Scènes de la vie de bohème*, translated as *The Latin Quarter* by Ellen Marriage and John Selwyn (London: Greening, 1908), pp.xxvi-xxviii.

[5] Quoted by Sherill Tippins, *February House* (London: Pocket Books, 2006), p.248.

ever lived.' The Soviet regime feared the 'uncontainable' in his music, tried to contain it 'whether by denunciation or adulation, coercion or cajolery, censorship or co-option,' though never by 'neglect or indifference.'[6] How did that affect it? Did the suffering the regime caused the composer indeed improve his music? 'Millions of people, the flower of the nation,' lived under the regime, 'vacillating,' as Levon Hakobian puts it, 'between fairly understandable and conscious conformism and an awareness of being constantly faced with something alien, objectionable, and sinister.' That 'engendered an extraordinarily rich psychological background for every kind of reflection on the ultimate and most profound metaphysical questions.'[7]

What is certain is that audiences responded to his works, which, by demonstrably sharing their ambivalence, in a measure redeemed their suffering. 'For many of us,' a Russian *emigré* said, 'listening to a new piece by Shostakovich was a sacred experience.'[8] 'He could not disregard the inner deception of our existence,' Victor Bobrovsky wrote, 'the pain he experienced for us all, for our spiritual impurity, for the daily desecration of the truth, this was what summoned his muse to life.'[9]

If artists can achieve that, can others? Perhaps artists are fortunate inasmuch as their creativity may be shared, its power redoubled. Is suffering creative for others? Or, at least, can it be made so? Most of us are aware that some suffering is often a condition of achievement: we agonisingly practise, we train, we are nervous before we go on stage, give a lecture, make a speech; and many would argue that what we do is better as a

---

[6] Richard Taruskin, 'When serious music mattered,' in *A Shostakovitch Casebook*, ed. Malcom Hamrick Brown (Bloomington: Indiana University Press, 2005), p.372.

[7] Levon Hakobian, 'A Perspective on Soviet Musical Culture during the Lifetime of Shostakovitch,' in *A Shostakovitch Casebook*, p.226.

[8] Quoted by Paul Mitchinson, 'The Shostakovitch Variations,' in *A Shostakovitch Casebook*, p.318.

[9] Quoted by Ludmila Kovnatskaya, 'Dialogues about Shostakovitch,' in *A Shostakovitch Casebook*, p.250.

result – our performance has an edge, an excitement. Less obvious, perhaps, is the possibility that such achievement, though attained with some suffering, holds at bay, if it does not defeat, the deeper suffering brought by the fear of loneliness and, deeper yet, the dread of death.

Such arguments are offered by Moulyn, and are surely to be placed in the context of a yet more recent historical trend. On the one hand, advances in biotechnology suggest a yet more mechanistic and deterministic approach to the mysteries of the human condition. On the other hand, advances in medical science, in particular in the invention and use of drugs, make it possible to eliminate some of the sources of suffering and to reduce the pain of other sorts. We live longer. But some live only part of a life, numbed by drugs, demented in old age. In the late twentieth century, as Joanna Bourke puts it, 'not only was the soul absent from deathbed considerations, the body itself was hooked to a machine that took precedence over the free will of the dying person The medicalisation of death finally stripped the Beyond of both heaven and hell, leaving dying people with little to ward off their fears of annihilation.'[10] Is it death that is to be dreaded or an unintelligent existence? Has suffering been unnecessarily prolonged? Who is to say?

I take it that there is, as a result, a number of arguments in the medical and caring professions which others can conduct better than historians, or at least this historian. But I cannot help wondering whether Moulyn's answer is more than a partial one. 'Even lower if all suffering had some beneficial office, it would still be impossible to defend the amount of suffering that exists,' writes John Laird. 'Cancer may give an occasion for fortitude and for a certain melancholy dignity, but, in its case, anodynes are better than dignity and most of the suffering is sheer waste.'[11]

In extreme circumstances – such as the death camps – some have been able to resort to creativity, both prompted by and assuaging their suffering, and Moulyn writes of 'sagas of

---

[10] J. Bourke, *Fear* (London: Virago, 2005), pp.320-321.

[11] John Laird in Robert N. Fisher *et al.*, *Suffering, Death and Identity* (Amsterdam: Rodopi, 2002), p.30.

creative people who do not give in and do not give up.' He advocates 'the heroic life-style.'[12] But while he is at pains to suggest that the concept does not apply only to Socrates or Beethoven, we cannot help wondering whether we can hope to live up to it, and whether, even if we have kept loneliness at bay by albeit painful creativity, we shall be able to cope with the dread of death, the end of subjective time, and, perhaps, the end, so far we are concerned, of objective time as well.

Yet another recent change, at least in part a connected one, may be signalled by the historian. We have increased our capacity to recall; we have also increased our recourse to 'memory.' It is, of course, nothing new to honour ancestors, to remember the dead, to set up memorials, to find that place evokes past. Maybe, however, we now go further, substituting human memory for God's enumeration.

Visiting the family home, the great early twentieth century Polish composer Karol Szymanowski heard it 'whisper, quietly telling the tale of days long ago.' He listened: did he not hear his father's voice? 'That evening, I realised that people do not completely die; the sweet shades of their words and smiles become for ever one with everything which surrounded them in life – one has only to know how to summon the dead and to hear what they have to say.'[13]

Robert Fisher writes that 'The lower vanishing of people we love, forever, is not an easy thing to continue to live with. But we can give their lives and their dying meaning by letting go, letting go because of what the person has meant to us, and because we love that person for the memory of what he or she continues to mean for us. That is the hope we can give to the suffering of those we love. This is a way of redeeming suffering.'[14]

Fisher is writing of those we know and love and of the risk that we prolong their suffering though hope is lost. Yet what of those we have never known and might have found it impossible to love? Perhaps that is the point of memorials, of

---

[12] Moulyn, *The Meaning of Suffering*, pp.195, 289.

[13] Quoted by A. Wightman, *Karol Szymanowski* (Aldershot: Ashgate, 1999), p.53.

[14] Fisher *et al.*, *Suffering, Death and Identity*, p.73.

'sites' of memory, even though they may be constructed in a spirit of vainglory.

The historian before you is not a music historian, whether that is obvious or not, but a political one, in particular an historian of imperialism and international relations. Though it may be his dearest wish, the historian, as J.A. Froude recognized, cannot hope to enter the mind of others. The motivation even of the heroes remains obscure. What can the historian hope to say about the sufferings of those who fought in wars or suffered tortures? Only a little, and rather generalised. To some extent, it may be that the fear of loneliness overcame the dread of death. Men risked death together.

They also created other worlds of meaning. The enforced submission of Cambodia to reunited Nguyen Vietnam, along with increased *corvée* and Vietnamese colonization, prompted rebellion in the eastern provinces in 1820-1821, led by a monk called Kai. He 'washed the heads of his soldiers, reciting sutra to give them strength, and shaking drops of water on to them to keep the Vietnamese from dispersing them in battle. If the Vietnamese fired guns, the power of the Khmer would keep the bullets from going far or coming close to them. When Kai's blessings were over, his soldiers lost their apathy, and went out to battle the Vietnamese'.[15] That may seem incomprehensible, until we recall the men who went away to war in 1914.

In the Philippines, which had not known Buddhism, nor, for the most part, Islam, such popular attitudes took on Christian features. As Rafael Ileto has shown, the dramatized epic of Christ's resurrection helped to shape a view of the world that fused elements of the remote past and of the introduced religion. A Kristo was a man of power, lowly and humble, but superior to the priests of the establishment. To die for his cause was to see Heaven. Maybe here we see a popular version of the 'creativity' of which Moulyn writes. Certainly, we can see an elite version in the Spanish

---

[15] 1869 poem, quoted by D. Chandler, 'An Anti-Vietnamese Rebellion in Nineteenth Century Cambodia,' *Journal of Southeast Asian Studies* 6 (1975), p.21.

Philippines. There elements of the elite identified the suffering of the people and identified with the people. The same happened in Europe. Dimitry Karakozov wondered 'why my beloved simple Russian people has to suffer so much! ... why next to the eternal simple peasant and the labourer in his factory and workshop are there people who do nothing, idle nobles, a horde of officials and other wealthy people, all living in shining houses?... The man really responsible is the Tsar.'[16]

He would kill the Tsar, Alexander II, and die for the people. He tried in vain. Years later another was to succeed and kill others as well. For Mazzini, the nation had displaced God: it was [again] beautiful to die pro patria mori. For Ben Anderson, it is too impoverished an idea to justify such sacrifice. Why have so many died for 'such limited imaginings'?[17]

Attempting to create a unified nation, Indonesian leaders pictured a community of suffering under the Dutch, shared for 300 years, though in fact Dutch rule had not extended so far for so long.

For others Christianity provided a metaphor, a powerful one, though clearly not the only possible one. It was, of course, strongest of all in the Philippines, Christianized from the late sixteenth century onwards. The great nationalist polymath, Jose Rizal came, it seems, to construct his life as a sacrifice, giving it meaning by seeking or accepting martyrdom.

'Alas, Jose!' a townmate wrote to him in 1889. 'All the people here ask about you and pin their hope on you. Even the poorest people of the mountains are asking about your return. It seems that they consider you the second Jesus who will liberate them from misery!'[18] He returned to the Philippines, was arrested, and, when the Katipunan revolt

---

[16] F. Venturi, *Roots of Revolution* (London: Weidenfeld and Nicolson, 1960), pp.345-346.

[17] Benedict Anderson, *Imagined Communities* (London and New York: Verso, 1991), p.7.

[18] Quoted by R. Ileto, *Pasyon and Revolution* (Quezon City: Ateneo de Manila University Press, 1979), p.313.

broke out in 1896, was executed.

> Land of my idolatry, my misery of miseries,
> Beloved Philippines, hear this last farewell.
> I give you now my all, my parents, all I have loved.
> I go to where there are no slaves, no hangmen, no oppressors,
> Where faith does not slay, where he who reigns is God.[19]

Nationalism, the nation state, and the relations among nation-states continue to construct our lives. They construct deaths, too, including the death of those in the past, who were or may be retroactively made members of a nation. The Second World War produced great suffering. After the first war, the discourse was of guilt; after the second of apology, and subsequent globalisation has expanded it. The suffering caused by disease and dementia remains a mystery, no easier to explain or accept than it was. For the suffering inflicted by human beings on other human beings, apology is possible. Even in the case of individuals, however, its redemptive character may be undermined by inadequacy or by suspicion of insincerity. Apologising for the actions of a people, or the majority of a people, or a government that may have acted for it, must surely be still more questionable, particularly if those who suffered are dead, and those who are apologising, or on whose behalf apology is being tendered, were not themselves involved. Sincerity may not be obliterated. But it is hard to avoid the conclusion that such apologies may have additional, if not alternative, purposes. Apology, sometimes accompanied by monetary payment, may be designed to shape consensus within the nation-state, for whom the past is often a source of legitimation. It may be designed to improve relations with another nation-state.

The first President Bush apologized in 1990 for the incarceration of Japanese Americans at the outset of the Pacific war. In 2002 the Clark government in New Zealand apologized for the discriminatory poll tax levied on early

---

[19] Quoted by Austin Coates, *Rizal, Philippine Nationalist and Martyr* (Hong Kong: Oxford University Press, 1968), p.323.

Chinese settlers in New Zealand. The main focus of the discourse has, however, been on German and Japanese actions in the 1930s and 1940s, and more particularly on the Japanese. Meeting the President of Korea in 1990 Prime Minister Kaifu Toshiki apologized in respect of the 'unbearable grief and suffering' caused by 'the actions of our country,' and Miyazawa Kiichi repeated the words in 1992.[20] But, for Japan, as Yamazaki puts it, 'the apology has become a ritual of remorse that ... has yet to reach its potential in providing reconciliation with the past, with its neighbours and with the international community.'[21]

Perhaps academics should not be too hard on such politicians, for there is a risk, too, in their activities, even though they focus on explanation rather than expiation. 'Academics observe, analyse, and try to explain human behaviour. In so doing ... we exploit the experience, and even perhaps, the suffering of others.' In our attempts to explain, as Yamazaki says, 'we distance ourselves and the reader from truly recognizing the suffering and wrongdoing of our subjects. In explaining, we somehow explain away.'[22] There is another risk, however, one that, say, James Warren does not avoid in his fascinating alternative histories of Singapore, his account of the rickshaw coolies, for example: the work comes to seem sentimental, the author preachy. [23] Perhaps there is no better way, at least for the historian, than trying to tell it as it was, and evoking memory, stimulating reflection, rather than calling for apology.

This chapter was first published in Perspectives on Human Suffering, *edited Jeff Malpas and Norelle Lickiss (Dordrecht: Springer, 2012).*

---

[20] Jane W. Yamazaki, *Japanese Apologies for World War II: a rhetorical study* (London: Routledge, 2006), pp.42, 60.

[21] Ibid., p.139.

[22] Ibid., p.viii.

[23] James F. Warren, *Rickshaw Coolie a people's history of Singapore* (Singapore: Oxford University Press, 1986).

3. On Hope

'And now abideth, faith, hope and charity, these three; but the greatest of these is charity.'[1] Hope is one of the three graces, though not the greatest, which is charity, compassion or love. Hope 'exists', but, though it has been personified, and Oscar Wilde's mother was called (but not named) Speranza, it exists only in human thought and feeling. There, indeed, it makes a frequent appearance, widely and variously employed. Cause or effect, that suggests its many ambiguities. And those are expanded by its verbal and adjectival forms, also widely and variously employed. A grace, it sounds beneficent, but it may not be so.

The word may be used or abused in quite a quotidian way. I hope the weather will be fine; I hope the traffic is not too bad; I hope the soufflé rises, the jelly turns out, the toast does not burn, the seminar succeeds. But I think, it is my hope, that we are considering its use on rather grander occasions. We may hope for peace, for forgiveness, for redemption, for health, recovery, survival. But while the grace has a halo of goodness and beneficence, it is also possible for human beings to invoke it for other purposes. Human beings have hoped to assassinate their rulers, to destroy their enemies, to 'cleanse' their territories, though presumably with anticipated advantage or betterment in mind.

Its relationship with action is also ambiguous. Is it a substitute for it or is it a stimulus? The grace is associated not only with aspiration but also in a measure with expectation. That may prompt us to do little: we can only hope. It may prompt us to do a great deal, even engage in a last hope or support a forlorn hope. But it may also suggest a lack of expectation: living in hopes suggests a doubtful prospect.

We may use it of and for ourselves, but we may also use it of others. We can be somewhat godlike, co-opt the grace, take on a responsibility. One can give hope to others as well as or perhaps more than to oneself, even 'raise their hopes' too high. One can also deprive others of hope, dash their hopes, making them face harsh reality, disillusionment, even reducing

---

[1] St Paul, *First Epistle to the Corinthians*, ch.13, verse 13

them to despair. Hell is without hope. Abandon Hope all ye who enter here, as Orpheus is bidden by Speranza in the Danteesque words of Striggio that Monteverdi set in one of the first Italian operas.

Adjectivally the concept can be used descriptively, even judgmentally. She's one of the young hopefuls, we may say: a phrase indicating a rather patronising or equivocal form of approval. He's hopeless, we may add, indicating not that he is without his hopes, his aspirations, but that we have no hopes of him, no expectations.

If all these usages refer to individuals, they may of course also be applied to groups, even, perhaps, whole societies. A leader may give a group hope, misleading or not, motivate his or her followers, lead them to share his or her aspirations, mobilise them for good or evil purpose. 'The day may dawn when fair play, love for one's fellow men, respect for justice and freedom, will enable tormented generations to march forth serene and triumphant from the hideous epoch in which we have to dwell', were Churchill's retirement words in 1955. 'Meanwhile, never flinch, never weary, never despair.'[2] It helps if there seems to be no other hope, but also if there is a reward, temporal or spiritual, for the individual and the group, a promised land, sighted from Pisgah; a place in Heaven itself.

How can a historian hope to deploy this widely used and ambiguous word? It can surely be used — must be? — if he or she is writing of an individual. That person may indeed express hope or hopes; there may be other hopes less openly avowed. If the historian had any hope of understanding what he or she does and to offer any kind of explanation of it, he or she will want to discover and explore those hopes, those aspirations and expectations, though, as E.H. Carr argued,[3] it will not be sufficient to enquire why individuals, in their own estimation, acted as they did.

---

[2] Winston Churchill, 1.3.1955 (last speech in the House of Commons), available at *International Churchill Society*, 'Speeches, 1946-1963: Elder Statesman', https://winstonchurchill.org/resources/speeches/1946-1963-elder-statesman/never-despair/ (accessed July 2020).

[3] *What is History?* (Harmondsworth: Penguin, 1961), pp.48ff.

The historian, moreover, is not, or not simply, a biographer. He or she deals also with the movements of groups, with the changes within and among societies. Inasmuch as hope moves individuals, it also moves groups: indeed, a leader may spread it among them. The historian's account will take account of it and seek to analyse its role. It is also a matter of time. Can an 'age' be described as a 'Time of Hope', — to borrow the title of a C.P. Snow novel [did he borrow it?] — or an 'Age of Anxiety'? — to borrow the title of a Bernstein symphony. Or does such a generalisation fall short of or go beyond explanation?

The historian and the biographer may hope to find many instances in which hope has inspired his or her subjects, for it is surely a motive for the actions he or she describes. One that springs to my mind derives from my work on the Raj of Sarawak in the nineteenth century. Could this polity, created by a private adventurer, Sir James Brooke, survive without securing the protection of a recognised state? The founder thought it could not, and, failing to secure the protection of Britain, was prepared to turn to others, even the neighbouring Dutch. His nephew, Brooke Johnson Brooke, administering the raj, looked to succeed to its burden, its risk and its glory. 'Dear dear Raja, your extreme despondency is the effect of a debilitated constitution – it is not warranted by the state of things here for God's sake don't go and give away to either English, Dutch or America – the country you have won with your blood, with your fortune and with your life's labour. Don't give away from me and my children the inheritance you have promised us.'[4] To add to the nephew's near despair, his wife died in giving birth to a second son, whom he named Hope.[5] That suggested that his letter to the Raja was not merely attempted persuasion: hope was his own motive. He seems to have felt it in a rather desperate way even at this point. Desperation was indeed to overcome his sense of reality. He challenged the Raja in 1862 and he and his family were deprived of the succession. If hope can motivate action,

[4] Tarling, *Burden, the Risk and the Glory* (Oxford: Oxford University Press, 1982), p.244

[5] Ibid, p.245

so, it seems, can loss of it. Does desperation, however, imply its complete loss? Or is there a residue of hope within it?

Within the limits of wealth and power and position, Brooke Johnson Brooke was a free man, able at least to attempt to act on his motives, to attempt to realise his hopes. What role does hope play in narratives of the imprisoned? The objective of the captors is to deprive the captives of hope. Why? To prevent their escape? To 'break' them? To indulge their own power? To set an example? To secure 'confession' or 'information'? Their hopes may be dashed by counter-hopes. Prisoners have been able to sustain themselves on the slimmest diet of hope, sometimes, it seems, on a diet of mere endurance. Those of us who have not suffered the deprivation of liberty may find it difficult to understand and recognise that we could not do it ourselves, and certainly not emerge from captivity, if we did, with anything like the generosity of spirit, the realised and continued hope, of a Nelson Mandela.

Identifying with the left-wing [LEKRA], the great Indonesian novelist Pramoedya Ananta Toer spent many years in prison on the island of Buru under the Suharto regime. His papers were taken or destroyed on his arrest, and initially he had no writing materials on Buru. He told his fellow prisoners the story that became the great tetralogy *This Earth of Mankind*,[6] only written down after 1975 when he was allowed to use a battered typewriter.

Undoubtedly the ability to tell the story and then to write it helped to sustain Pramoedya, and his fellow-prisoners, but is that hope? One hardly needs to imagine conditions, like solitary confinement, when even such an activity was impossible, and, like Terry Waite in Lebanon, one could only rehearse stories in one's own mind. Is such activity hope? Perhaps it at least suggests that there is hope, so that it seems worthwhile to go on. And, of course, we do not need to imagine, though it is difficult fully to comprehend, the endurance of those few who survived the death camps of the Third Reich.

---

[6] Pramoedya Ananta Toer, *This Earth of Mankind*, trans. Max Lane (Harmondsworth: Penguin, 1996, [1980]).

What if there is no hope? in, say, the mad and murderous jail of Tuol Sleng in Cambodia. Primo Levi observed and wrote down what he saw at Auschwitz, destroyed the writing but remembered what he wrote. It wore him down but bore him up. But what if you were without the skill that education had given him? Levi tells us of an innocent Hungarian, Bandi, a newcomer or *Zugang* swept into the camp when Hitler took over his country, who initially worked with a will and refused to lie and steal. The author reads him a letter he has received through an Italian 'free' labourer, translating it into German, though neither he nor Bandi know the language well. 'But he understood what was essential for him to understand: that that piece of paper represented a breach, a small gap in the black universe that closed tightly around us, and through that breach hope could pass.' That he understood it, or sensed it, seemed to be shown when he rummaged in his pocket and 'with loving care, pulled out a radish'. He gave it to Levi: 'This is for you. It's the first thing I've stolen.'[7]

Some, of course, may have a faith that gives this hope. Levi, Carole Angier tells us, had faith 'in knowledge, and in man to make us of it.'[8] Others had an older faith. 'Jesus comes to us as One unknown, without a name, as of old by the lakeside He sets us to the tasks which He has to fulfil for our time. He commands. And to those who obey Him, whether they be wise or simple, He will reveal Himself in the toils, the conflicts, the sufferings which they shall pass through in His fellowship, and, as an ineffable mystery, they shall learn in their own experience who He is.'[9]

So individualistic and mystical a hope sufficed for Albert Schweitzer, and sustained his [albeit controverted?] life of service. It cannot be enough for everyone, even if they are free enough (and complicated enough?) to see things in this way.

---

[7] 'A Disciple', in Primo Levi, *Moments of Reprieve: A Memoir of Auschwitz*, trans. Ruth Feldman (London: Abacus, 1987), p.54

[8] Carol Angier, *The Double Bond: Primo Levi: A Biography* (London: Viking, 2002), p.302

[9] Albert Schweitzer, *The Quest of the Historical Jesus*, See my notes p.401

Others, indeed, put find their hope in a faith, both simpler and more complicated? - that transcends this world. The trumpet shall sound. We shall die but not die. Christ's promise is of resurrection. God will [again] intervene in history, 'and there shall be no more death, neither sorrow, nor crying, neither shall there be any more pain'.[10] But, if we are in a position to do anything besides draw comfort — what are we to do meanwhile?

The existentialist Rudolf Bultmann argued that we cannot now believe in that kind of intervention. 'The man who complains "I cannot see meaning in history, and therefore my life, woven into history, is meaningless" is to be told "do not look around you into universal history, but look into your own personal history, always in your present lies the meaning of history; you cannot see this as a spectator, but you can realize it in your responsible decisions.'[11] Is this very far from Schweitzer? Translated into twentieth century expectation, the gospel promised the individual 'new life here and now, a life which, in response to the word about Christ, has new purpose, direction and power'.[12] But what does this offer to someone shut up in a prison and in no position to take responsible decisions?

Influenced by the Marxist Ernst Bloch, Jurgen Moltmann thought that the Bultmann approach skewed the Gospel. No human beings, he argued, could be content with their own existence without holding out hope for others.[13] But could not Bultmann's line include holding out hope for others and doing something for them. 'Belief in God's promise that things can and will be different is just what is needed to spur us to action in the present.' We should not accept that nothing will get better; 'those who hope in Christ can no longer put up with

---

[10] *The Bible*, King James version, *Revelation*, ch 21, v.4

[11] Quoted in Norman Young, 'Hope, Faith and Action', in C. Mostert (ed), *Hope Challenging the Culture of Despair* (Adelaide: ATF Press, 2004), p.75]

[12] Norman Young, *Creator, Creation and Faith* (London: Collins, 1976), p.76.

[13] Quoted ibid., p.77.

reality as it is, but begin to suffer under it, to contradict it.'[14] 'God is at work in the World wherever there are those being liberated whom Jesus lived and died to liberate, those with whom he identified himself in his life and death, the poor, the oppressed, the alienated and the godless.'[15] Christian hope must 'bring the hoped-for future into practical contact with the misery of the present.'[16]

Hope, indeed, may sustain the individual, give comfort, sustain inaction, encourage action where possible. But it extends to others, as with Schweitzer and I suppose after all Bultmann. It can be brought to them. It can be drawn from them. They may be desperate for it, and you may be anxious for their support. Hope may inspire leaders, and inspire others to follow them, their charisma drawing on their power of prophecy. It is a matter for groups as well as individuals.

It is in such a context that millennial movements might be placed. Those, common in East and Southeast Asia, are not, of course, peculiar to it. They are sometimes deemed to be irrational. It might be better be said that they operate within a rationality peculiar to their society and their situation. They appear in societies and situations that appear to offer no other route to change, no other way of improving one's lot. The movements often try to recapture an apparently better past or to pre-empt a happier future or both. They are inspired by prophecy, by trust, by charisma, by hope. 'Millenarian movements [in Java]', Sartono Kartodirdjo writes, 'even though religious in a sense, were not other-worldly. They were concerned with rational goals pertaining to this world even if the goals were not rationally perceived. Or, to put it differently, they were concerned with goals which were rational within the framework of an existing world-view.'[17]

Such movements appeared in colonial societies, but were not peculiar to them. The Little Tradition in China comprises

---

[14] J. Moltmann, *The Theology of Hope* (London: SCM, 1967), p.21, quoted in Young, *Creator, Creation and Faith*, p.77.

[15] Quoted in Young, *Creator, Creation and Faith*, p.821.

[16] Ibid., p.148.

[17] *Protest Movements in Rural Java* (Singapore: Oxford University Press, 1973), p.17.

a strong element of millenarianism, and so do the *yonaoshi* or world renewal movements in Japan, and of course they appear in European history, too. In pre-colonial Vietnam, again, the Little Tradition might challenge the Great. In the Tran Cao rebellion of 1516, the leader claimed descent from a previous dynasty, declared himself the incarnation of Indra, and also claimed to be fulfilling a popular prophecy. The *Kha* 'rebellion' against Siamese authority in Champassak in 1819 was led by a renegade monk who claimed magical powers.

We know more about such movements in the colonial phase, since there are better records, and maybe, too, they were more frequent, for alien rule was more obvious, and the chance of securing change in other ways even less. Prince Diponegoro embodied 'the widespread millenarian expectations of the time and made himself the focus of the ideals and longings which gripped the Javanese countryside before the outbreak of the war'[19] in Java in 1825 This was the Age of Wrath, and the appearance of cholera and the eruption of Merapi in 1822, surely heralded the reign of the *Ratu Adil*, the just prince.

In the Philippines, by contrast, millennial movements took on Christian overtones. Spain had 'christianized' its people, but the popularization of Catholicism gave it a life outside the institutions the Spaniards set up. The propagation of Christ's teachings, through hymns, poems and dramas, and, as Reynaldo Ileto has convincingly shown, the dramatized epic of His passion, death and resurrection, helped to reshape the popular view of the World, and of its possible transformation. A *Kristo* was a man of power, lowly and humble, but superior in knowledge to the priests of the establishment. To die for his cause was to see heaven.

Even now, however, millennial movements were not confined to colonial territories. Siam escaped colonial rule, though adopting many of its practices. In 1889 Phraya Phahon's rebellion in Chiang Mai was directed against the enforcement of Bangkok's rule in the north. A petty official linked to Chiang Mai royalty, he was able to mobilise 3000 peasant followers by articulating their discontent in a popular religious idiom. Invulnerable, a man of extraordinary powers, he was expected to reign as the ideal 'Buddhist king' and lead a revitalized Chiang Mai independent of Bangkok and freed of the burden of taxation.

Millenarianism in Europe was not confined to the medieval and early modern periods. Marx sought to contend with utopianism. He urged a 'scientific' approach that took account of historical trends and practical realities. Yet even he retained a residue of utopianism. 'He had simply thrust the happy consummation a little farther off into the future.'[18] There was still hope: the workers would triumph; the state would wither away. But you would have to work for it, cooperating with the forces of history.

The historian may hope to deploy hope as part of an explanation of events: it activates individuals; and [as a result] it enables leaders to motivate groups, individuals strengthened in their hope by a sense of community and by the conviction and charisma a leader may convey. May the historian go further and apply the word to a whole society, a state, an age? In general it would be to over-generalize. But there is something in it. '"Hopeless, but not serious" was the guiding principle which the age of Baroque stamped upon the Habsburg world', wrote A.J.P. Taylor.[19] Fatalism certainly affected the decisions its leaders made in 1914. 'We were bound to die', Czernin declared.[20] The same gloom penetrated *fin-de-siecle* Italy. Cavaradossi in Puccini's opera *Tosca* [1900] dies despairing, bereft of consolation. And that was not merely an expression of Puccini's own melancholy.[21]

And what of the early twenty-first century? 'To think about hope today is to do so in a disillusioned age, an age of no great hope or at least of a pervasive sense that hope is not really justifiable. A culture of despair is not concealed very deeply below the preoccupation with the demands of daily life and

---

[18] Edmund Wilson, *To the Finland Station* (Garden City, N.Y.: Doubleday, 1940), p.334.

[19] Taylor, *The Habsburg Monarchy* (London: Hamish Hamilton, 1948), p.12.

[20] Quoted ibid., p.232.

[21] Franco Serpa in William Weaver (ed), *The Puccini Companion* (New York: Norton, 1994), p.102.

the obsession with being entertained', writes Christiaan Mostert.[22]

The millennium, as he points out, was approached with anticipation [a year early, indeed], with parties and fireworks, but also with some anxiety:[23] Would our world crash with our computers, the clocks stop, the planes drop out of the sky? There was arguably less optimism around in 2000 than in 1900. Then there was, if not in Austria, Hungary or Italy, a wide belief in 'progress'. Within less than a generation, however, Europe was engaged in the 'Great War', and, a generation later, the whole World engaged in a second war in which perhaps 70-80 million died. The power of the myth of progress is now, for most of us, the haunting power of its ghost', write Bauckham and Hart.[24] 'The twentieth century has drained almost all the life out of it, but it has so dominated and permeated the culture of modernity we cannot easily leave it behind' though 'much more certain of its ambiguity than its inevitability'.[25] That meant the collapse of one grand narrative. Marx's own version has collapsed, too. Postmodernism denied their possibility. There were only 'stories', little stories, indeed. 'If we can find meaning neither in the myth of progress nor in any "grand narrative", the tempting alternative is to seek distraction and entertainment. ... What basis for hope can be found in mere hedonism and a disillusioned pragmatism?'[26] Is that putting it the wrong way round? Are they not the result of loss of hope? Is it now possible to 'live in hope'? Can hope survive in a secular world? Must there be a 'wager on transcendence', a 'hope against hope', a belief in a God who created the world and 'intends, in a way and at a

---

[22] Mostert, *Hope Challenging the Culture of Despair*, p.49

[23] Ibid., p.53.

[24] Richard Bauckham and Trevor Hart, *Hope against Hope: Christian Eschatology at the Turn of the Millennium* (Grand Rapids, Eerdmans, 1999)., p.7, quoted by Mostert, *Hope Challenging the Culture of Despair*, p.54

[25] Mostert, *Hope Challenging the Culture of Despair*, p.541.

[26] Ibid., p.541.

time not in our control, something glorious for it and with it'?[27]

Unable to place that bet, I am yet unwilling to see 'hope' itself commodified, though forms of it have often been sold. Should it become merely a management tool in our consumer society? Even I, though somewhat inured after writing, with Wilf Malcolm, a book on modern universities,[28] to the crass nature of management literature, was surprised by Andrew Razeghi's *Hope*. 'From shrinking product life cycles to binge-and-purge hiring and firing, the world isn't going to get easier to manage. We need hope not only to cure what ails us but also for its performance benefits. When used appropriately, hope yields tangible benefits, from enhancing creativity to improving problem-solving skills. However, hope's primary benefit is its ability to give meaning in meaningless moments.'[29] The book has a sub-title: *how triumphant leaders create the future*: 'It is a leader's responsibility to create the conditions under which hope can manifest itself among a team';[30] 'Leaders personify hope.'[31]

Yet I suppose others have to deploy hope in order to 'manage' fellow human beings. That brings me back to the individual discussing whose hope I began this essay and whom I have tried to place in a larger social and temporal context. What hope should givers of hope give in an age without hope or where hope may only be a managerialist's tool? Perhaps it will depend on the individuals involved. What hope can we give a prisoner of conscience? What hope should we give a criminal prisoner? Will someone who is dying welcome a 'wager'? What should he or she be told? A doctor may know the patient, know whether he or she would prefer

---

[27] Ibid., p.66.
[28] Wilf Malcolm and Nicholas Tarling, *Crisis of Identity? The Mission and Management of Universities in New Zealand* (Wellington, Dunmore Publishing, 2007).
[29] Andrew Razeghi , *Hope: How Triumphant Leaders Create the Future* (San Francisco: Jossey-Bass, 2006).
[30] Ibid., p.63.
[31] Ibid., p.85.

or be able to bear the truth. The doctor will not want to lie but may wish to forbear.

His doctors did not tell Sir Malcolm Sargent that he had incurable cancer: they thought telling him would kill him. He managed to get to the podium in the Albert Hall and told the Promenaders he would be there the following year. Two days later he was sitting up planning his programmes for 1968. 'You have got to tell him', Sylvia Darley, his long-term secretary, insisted. 'He's up there now with his music and it's not fair. If you don't say something I will.' The doctor told him, and he wept. Later he told Sylvia: 'Well, at least I can stop working now.' 'I have always prayed for a foreknowledge of death so that I can see my friends', he said. On his instructions, visitors were told not to speak of his condition. 'I can't say goodbye as it is so wearing for me and them. It is so much easier if I just say come again soon.' As he finally faltered, Sylvia Darley put on his recording of *The Dream of Gerontius*, where the Angel sings: 'Farewell, but not for ever! I will come and wake thee on the morrow.'[32]

[32] Richard Aldous, *Tunes of Glory* (London: Pimlico, 2002), pp.242-5

4. On Human Presence

We are all here, all 'present', but what it means to be here is an obscure thing, hard to penetrate or even think about. One way to begin, perhaps, is to try to contemplate non-presence.

Non-presence

You have present in me a Southeast Asian historian, bound to remind you of the demographic immaturity of the region. Thinly populated till recent times, maybe only 30m in 1830, but now perhaps 600m, but there are still areas of empty jungle. You might there see or hear no human, though other wildlife might be present. A twig crackles. A bird sounds out at the top of the foliage. Or silence, even a frightening one.

Elgar wrote of the source of his setting of the words 'I go before my Judge' in his Newman-based oratorio *The Dream of Gerontius*. He meant, he told Augustus Jaeger, to describe 'an indefinable feeling that there's more around you than you know: have you ever been in a pitch-dark room and *felt* the presence of people when you have no proof or knowledge that anyone is there. I *have* and it feels like that.'[1]

Ferdinand Hiller, his pupil, spied on Hummel to see his master at work, composing his Rondo in B minor. Hummel discovered him and said in mock anger: 'I thought, or more accurately, I felt that I was no longer alone.'[2]

Some find the non-presence of human beings a comfort, an excitement. They have climbed the top of the mountain as in Strauss's *Alpine Symphony* and are exhilarated by the prospect and also by their own achievement, though rarely done all on their own, any more than that of a Trans-Tasman swimmer. Others find it unbearable, particularly if they have lost a long-term companion. They may seek to communicate with them, or even imagine that they see them.

---

[1] Quoted in M. Kennedy, *Portrait of Elgar* (Oxford: Oxford University Press, 1968), p.85.

[2] Quoted in Mark Kroll, *Johann Nepomuk Hummel* (Lanham: Scarecrow Press, 2007), p.250.

Others find the non-presence of others a necessity. To create? —Mahler had a summer house for writing symphonies in, and Bernard Shaw had one at Ayot St Lawrence that could revolve to catch the sun, though the mechanism is now too rusty. To commune with the divine? – a hermit, a desert father, stylites. To reflect? – 'On the beach at night alone', Walt Whitman wrote, '… I think a thought of the clef of the universes and the future.'[3] Some have seclusion thrust upon them. – prison, solitary confinement – and the object is to break their spirit. Terry Waite was not even allowed a book.

Marooned on Juan Fernandez in 1704, Alexander Selkirk's life was not, it seems, as Daniel Defoe was to depict in *Robinson Crusoe*. He was brutalised. When found in 1709 he had more or less lost the power of speech, having 'so much forgot his Language for want of Use, we could scarce understand him'.[4]

You can choose to be solitary without being made so and being alone may not mean being lonely. But dying alone might be another matter. A pensioner, Michael Clarke, was thought to have been dead for a year before his body was recently found in a Wellington council flat, and only then because the flats were about to be demolished.[5]

In the Presence of Others

You may be rescued or let out of jail, surrounded by stigma or praise. You have to work your way back into the presence of others.

That may have been difficult in the first place. Normally you have a voice, but it is some time before you can use it for speaking or singing. Some are perhaps born shy: maybe it is also dependent on upbringing, at home, or in schools, or in other venues of socialisation. Why are we given dolls to play with? Why do we have animal toys and live pets of which [or whom] we are encouraged to take an anthropomorphic view?

---

[3] *Collected Poems*, p.260; memorably set in the second movement of Vaughan Williams' *A Sea Symphony*.

[4] Woodes Rogers, quoted in Bill Bell, 'Selkirk's silence', *Times Literary Supplement*, 18 March 2011, p.14.

[5] *New Zealand Herald*, 14 September 2011, p.A9.

Over 70% of respondents to a survey by Purina New Zealand thought pets had human-like emotions. Nearly half of the women who answered thought their pet communicated its feelings better than their partner.[6]

How do you get to know others? Various methods of introduction, depending on status and social practice: schools, birthday parties, formal introductions, name cards, name tags, IDs, senior citizen travel cards, licenses. Other means may be more forceful. The cops stop you. You are arrested. You are thrown into jail. None of the people you meet did you want to meet. Communication with others seems a rather arbitrary feature of life. You must learn when it is appropriate to speak and when not. A well-meant act may be interpreted as a predatory move. Some will refuse contact: incommunicado. I'm afraid he's at a meeting. Can I help?

Teaching is a form of communication. Some of it can be done without actual human contact. But in general, it requires and involves a human relationship, still recalling, even in modern times, something of the ancient mystery that allowed the teachers to be masters and still allows musicians to be maestri. Maori learning was passed on in this way. 'The *whakapapa* were maintained by tohunga, who were recognised as professional genealogists. Their teaching was conducted in secret, under rigidly prescribed rules.'[7] But it is not peculiar to Maori.

You might also recall a comment from a student in a small class under the composer Sterndale Bennett at the Royal Academy of Music in the London of the mid-nineteenth century. 'Over this group', Louis Napoleon Parker wrote, 'Sir Sterndale presided with a certain indefinable grace and dignity which marked him as being set apart, as, in short, a great man. … The influence of his mere external personality over the impressionable young artists who surrounded him is

---

[6] *North Shore Times* [Auckland], 12 May 2011.
[7] Ranginui Walker, *Nga Papa a Ranginui* (Harmondsworth: Penguin: 1996), p.23.

indescribable. I believe there was not one of us who would not gladly have died for him.'[8]

Expanding your contacts, you may become the member of a group devoted to scouting or climbing or gardening or contract bridge or underwater hockey or join a society or become a member of a gang. That brings order and rules into your life and definition into your relationships as well as peer pressures. But some contacts again can be arbitrary. You find yourself in a crowd. And crowds can, as they say, turn ugly, stampede, panic. Can you resist their hysteria? Are they going overboard and taking you with them? The police may pick on you anyway. 'It's a copycat thing', one psychologist commented on the looting in the London riots in August 2011. 'You know it's wrong but it's okay because other people are doing it.'[9]

Violence might be the result of body language: a rude gesture, an insolent smile, an eye contact. Language is spoken, but body language read, perhaps with dubious accuracy. Recall the illustration Sellars and Yeatman offer in *Garden Rubbish* of the Boy Scout with wide open face and loyal knees. Useful perhaps for MI5; but how confident can we be that we are not reading into, rather than merely reading? Willy Clayton, 'KLOD' of the Australian Communist Party, was, one contact reported, 'a shadowy figure' who 'wouldn't look at me when I was reporting'. Another observed that 'the mysterious quality in his work ... was mirrored in his face, which nearly always wore a furtive expression'.[10]

'Age's triumph resides in visual worship', Thomas Mann wrote of Michelangelo's erotic poetry in 1950. The day before he had been smitten by a handsome waiter in Zürich. 'World

---

[8] Quoted in Stephen Siek, *England's Piano Sage. The Life and Teachings of Tobias Matthay* (Lanham: Scarecrow Press, 2012), p.33.

[9] Russell Read, quoted in *New Zealand Herald*, 10 August 2011.

[10] Quoted in C. Andrew, *Defence of the Realm* (Harmondsworth: Penguin, 2010), p.371.

renown is wonderful', he wrote in his diary, 'but it cannot compare with the smile in his eyes.'[11]

The Power of 'Presence'

There is, indeed, another kind of human presence, pertaining to someone who is, as it were, more than merely here, but here with effect, contrived or not. Their aura may derive from their beauty, their competence, their position, their possession of power, religious or political or social. Ivone Kirkpatrick accompanied Sir Samuel Wilson to see Hitler during the Munich crisis. 'I gazed at him in fascination. During one of his many tirades I was unable to take my eyes off him and my pencil remained poised above the paper.'[12] Or perhaps from their demonstrable impact on your peers, perhaps with a little enhancement, as with the dazzling white uniform the handsome Lord Mountbatten wore when accepting the Japanese surrender in Singapore in September 1945.

The Berlin Philharmonic played at the party rally in Nürnberg in 1936. The government of the Reich sat in the front row. 'Suddenly the excitement died down and the audience rose in unison – the Führer entered.' The orchestra played Beethoven's Pastoral Symphony. 'The Führer stepped up to the podium. He greeted us with a fascinating warmth radiating from his persona. We sense the magnitude of the moment we are experiencing and in which we have been blessed to participate.'[13]

An opera or a concert may be given in the gracious presence of H.M. the Queen. The performer on the stage or in the concert hall may have a striking presence that seems to go beyond their competence. Hearing *Messiah* in Westminster Abbey at the end of the war, Britten was 'impressed immediately by the nobility and beauty of [Kathleen Ferrier's]

---

[11] Anthony Heilbut, *Thomas Mann: Eros and Literature* (London: Macmillan, 1996), pp.264-5.
[12] Quoted in Niall Ferguson, *The War of the World*, (Harmondsworth: Penguin, 2006), p.358n.
[13] Werner Buchholz, quoted in Misha Aster, *The Reich's Orchestra* (London: Souvenir Press, 2010), p.118.

presence, and by the warmth and deep range of her voice'.[14]
For Yehudi Menuhin Georges Enesco was the 'absolute. …
Apart from those ineffable qualities we gloss over with words
like "presence" and the mystic mantle my veneration threw
around him, his musical prowess was simply phenomenal.'[15]

It will communicate to other artists. Janet Baker described
rehearsing with the late Sir Charles Mackerras in *Maria
Stuarda*. 'My delight in the clearly defined and contrasting
rhythms of the Donizetti score immediately transferred itself
to him across the pit. I could see his body and shoulders react
to my voice as he caught my mood and reacted to it in his
own inimitable way.'[16]

And the audience will respond. Indeed, the performer will
respond in turn. Inside Sadlers Wells, Hugh Walpole wrote of
a revival of *The Mastersingers* in 1938, there was 'so much
enjoyment radiating from the stage and out to the audience
and back from the audience to the stage again.'[17] Ferrier,
wrote her accompanist, Gerald Moore, 'seemed to embrace
the audience as she saw it; her nostrils dilated with excitement,
her eyes sparkled with joy'.[18]

What was the secret of the early nineteenth-century opera-
singer Maria Malibran's greatness? Her voice? It thrilled.
'Malibran impresses you by her marvellous voice, but no one
sings like her', wrote Chopin. Her combination of discipline
and spontaneity, of technique and passion? 'I remember how
I wept in Bologna when I saw her Desdemona', cried the
Norwegian violinist Ole Bull. The effect on audiences? They
felt in the end united with her and enlarged by her. Her singing
seemed, said Lady Blessington, to 'emanate from a soul
thrilling with sublime emotion; and its deep harmony causes
mine to vibrate. … It haunts one for many succeeding hours.'

---

[14] Quoted in N. Cardus, *Kathleen Ferrier A Memoir* (London;
Hamish Hamilton, 1954), p.54.

[15] Yehudi Menuhin, *Unfinished Journey* (London: Macdonald
and Jane's, 1977), p.70.

[16] Quoted in Susie Gilbert, *Opera for Everybody* (London:
Faber, 2009), p.335.

[17] Quoted in ibid., p.63.

[18] Quoted in Cardus, *Kathleen Ferrier A Memoir*, p.86.

And the applause? 'Delight beamed from her eyes', wrote another who had come under her spell; '... it was certainly the happiest moment in her life. And was it not also the happiest of mine? I shared in her delight as well as in the acclamation of the others.'[19]

Some modern musicians prefer to make records when an audience is present, and insist that their performance is enhanced. Recordings, the baritone Christopher Maltman claims, 'remain facsimiles of great events, dulling the extra dimensions of human communication which elevate mere singing into art'. Live recording 'represents a happy medium, if you'll forgive the pun. ... Sixteen years into my career I can say without doubt that it is only under true battle conditions that musical expression can truly blossom.'[20] Others fear an individual eye contact, as did Elizabeth Söderström. Looking at an audience member and finding he is reading the paper is discouraging, as indeed I found when lecturing at the University of Auckland. The audience is, however, part of the performance, even though it is coughing and rustling its programmes and chocolate wrappings. Be glad it is not eating potato crisps.

Some artists seem simply terrified. One, perhaps surprisingly, is the great Argentine pianist, Martha Argerich. 'Audiences are not important for me now and they never were. I have reached a stage when now I am even more terrified of house concerts where the public is near. If I have to play when they are close, then I am quite afraid.'[21] Why is the laughter and applause of a studio audience needed for a BBC comedy show?

Putting it on record – in the way Edison made possible – transformed not only the business of music but its performance and its reception, too. You could repeat a performance, though it never changed as it would in real life. You could hear the voice of the dead. And now you can hear

---

[19] Howard F. Bushnell, *Maria Malibran: a Biography of the Singer* (University Park: Pennsylvania State University Press, 1979), pp.171, 105.

[20] *Gramophone*, June 2011, p.23.

[21] Interview, *Gramophone*, November 2008, p.38.

invented voices, telling you to turn right or left or, as you move on to the wrong motorway access, to make a U-turn at the earliest opportunity; as well as recorded messages, assuring you that your business is important to them, but delaying, beyond the range of patience, the opportunity of speaking to a rather more real person.

The combination of personal aura, theatrical presentation, audience response and crowd hysteria may be alarming. In *Scouting for Boys* Lord Baden-Powell slated football fans for 'learning to be hysterical as they groan and cheer in unison with their neighbours'.[22] A crowd can be worked up, as President Sukarno recognised in an independence day speech: 'I know that on this present 17 August [1962] you are all looking to me. And because I know that, I feel somewhat troubled because I am conscious of the size of the responsibility I hold.'[23]

As Hitler knew, too. Erik Levi notes 'the relative paucity of political speeches from the Nazi leaders that were issued on commercial recordings. That suggests to him 'a possible deep-seated fear that such material would lose its impact if divorced from the emotive surroundings of a public rally.'[24] The recordings of the rallies can still in fact carry something of the power of the occasion even without the theatrical visual presentation. But Churchill's tellingly constructed speeches, though delivered to relatively small audiences or to the microphone, are powerful, too.

Even without human presence, hysteria is still a possibility. Body language can, after all, be a restraint as well as an incitement. Its absence is, of course, marked in written and printed communication. Is the effect of such absence still more significant in the various forms of electronic communication that have emerged in the past 25 years? It is

[22] Quoted in Matthew Reynolds' review of Morna O'Neill and Michael Hart (eds.), *The Edwardian Sense*, *Times Literary Supplement*, 3 December 2010, p.316.

[23] Quoted in John Legge, *Sukarno*, (New York: Praeger, 1972).

[24] Erik Levi, *Music in the Third Reich* (Basingstoke: Macmillan, 1994), p.146.

easy to communicate with large numbers of people in an unrestrained way. And a kind of hysteria may emerge, even if the emails do not lead to live protest meetings. It was evident at the Seattle WTO meeting of 1999 that the Internet had globalised the logistics of mass protest, and, as Rosemary Righter put it, given single-issue pressure 'a spurious homogeneity'.[25]

Semi-Presence

Before that, of course, there were other kinds of what we might call 'semi-presence', though there are gradations of it. There are the characters the actor and singer represent, drawn by librettist and composer from life and contrivance. There is the presence of the writer of letters, in memory or imagination. There is also 'authorial presence': is an author addressing us as with Meredith or Eliot or Thackeray? Or as with Henry Kingsley, who chattily writes of his hero Charles Ravenshoe: 'I hope you will not be much disappointed in him. He was a very nice boy, if you remember, and you will see immediately that he has grown into a very nice young man indeed.'[26]

Or is his or her presence merely implied or presumed by the shaping of events and characters, the descriptions and the conversations, as in more modern novels and in plays? The authorial presence may after all be no more than a structural device, concealing as much as revealing the author's real role. Sculptors and painters also represent 'presence' of a kind. What was the purpose of all those Rembrandt and Repin self-portraits? Painters sometimes put themselves into a picture. Film followed. Photographs gave an impression of greater actuality, though it might be contrived. The role of the auteur could surely be all the stronger for its apparent absence. The same applied when movies followed.

Through the telephone, you could hear another voice, talk live to another person not in your presence, imagine them, or

[25] Reviewing Mike Moore, *A World without Walls*, *Times Literary Supplement*, 26 September 2003.

[26] Henry Kingsley, *Ravenshoe* (London: Everyman, 1905 [1862]), p.50.

renew your connexion with them. Or, like Proust, you could listen to the opera, even before 'broadcasts. That first became possible in 1881. 'It is certain that every person who hears for the first time a telephone is struck by surprise', wrote a contemporary commentator; 'this mysterious voice, which comes from so far, has something strange about it.'[27] At the Paris Exhibition of 1889 some were observed clapping as if they were there, and were ridiculed. 'What they saw – tubes coming out of the wall, and other visitors – had no relation to what they heard.'[28] The listener had to construct a visual reality to parallel the auditory reality. You can still get a ripple of applause in a cinema for a Metropolitan Opera film, but it will have no effect on the performance, such as Malibran or Ferrier would have welcomed.

You can also still see, it is almost as maddening as hearing them, people who gesture vigorously and stride up and down while on their cell-phone. But the importance of gesture has surely diminished. 'An old-fashioned Anglo-Saxon male can go through life with his hands in his pockets.'[29] He may be on the receiving end when blessed in church, or given out by a cricket umpire, or abused by an angry cyclist. But if Churchill's speeches were moving, his Victory-sign, like Hitler's salute, could be understood by even more.

In 1996 Howard Rheingold, 'doyen of the info-democrats', thought it 'amazing how the ambiguity of words in the absence of body language inevitably leads to online misunderstandings.[30] More recent electronic media go further. Skype allows you not only to see but to converse. Does body language come into use again? What effect does that have on the relationships involved? It contrasts greatly with the

---

[27] Quoted in Annegret Foster, *Musical Encounters at the 1889 Paris World's Fair* (Rochester, NY: Rochester University Press, 2005), p.289.

[28] Ibid., pp.288, 291.

[29] Ferdinand Mount, reviewing Angus Trumble, *The Finger*, *Times Literary Supplement*, 7 January 2011, p.7.

[30] Christopher May, *The Information Society A Sceptical View* (Cambridge: Polity, 2002), p.92.

exchange of letters or the long-distance and very brief and costly telephone calls of only a generation or so ago. It is amazing, a wonder. But does it risk taking some excitement out of life? Has it abolished expectation?

More serious, perhaps, is the risk of confusing actualities with non- or semi-actualities that the development of electronic media presents. The connexion between violence in the media and violent behaviour has long been a concern. Does a Tom-and-Jerry cartoon help to elide the effect of violence? Characters are flattened, but pop up again. Do computer games, offering a kind of actuality, obscure the *real* actuality? Perhaps they make it easier to think that violence is without effect. The victim will pop up again.

There are 'geeks' who no longer communicate with human beings, the *otaku* of the Japanese, 'obsessive fans who exchange the real world for closed-off, media-generated worlds'.[31] The newfangled means of communication are sometimes addictive. Are we 'killing deeper relationships'? Tracey Barnett, a columnist in the *New Zealand Herald* wonders. Losing social skills? Making more connexions, but shallower ones?[32]

Trust, we are told, plays a large part in our transactions, political and economic. In the Chinese world, it is said, it is the prime factor in sustaining commercial networks. Is it possible, a diplomat asks, to build trust without personal contacts? Is the familiarity of other forms of contact spurious?

Facebook indeed seems rather sad. At the end of 2010 it had more than 500 million active users. Its popularity is judged by the number of 'Facebook friends'. A Massey University student had 1047 and spent five hours a day on the site, the *New Zealand Herald* reported on 4 January 2011. Three days later the newspaper carried the report of a suicide. 'The mother of a woman who announced her intention to commit suicide to more than one thousand of her Facebook friends has angrily demanded why not one of them came to her

---

[31] Ian Condry, *Hip-hop Japan: Rap and the Paths of Cultural Globalization* (Durham, NC: Duke University Press, 2006), p.115.
[32] *New Zealand Herald*, 19 August 2011.

daughter's aid before she died.' 'Somebody could have helped', said a 'friend'. 'They were all posting how much they care for her but someone should have at least popped round to see that she was okay.'[33] A survey indicated that the average user in New Zealand had 124 friends, 'but that term should be applied loosely'. 70% of respondents were friends with people they had not seen since school, and 35% with people they had never met in person.[34]

Some like that kind of contact, even find it useful. 'I use the internet to chat with who[m]ever is on line', a student from Taiwan told an Australian survey. 'I don't care who they are as long as they don't know who I am … I get someone to talk to, and I can express myself. I also get my confidence, and I can practise my English as well.'[35] You can be less inhibited. The kind of 'inflation of sensibility' that may result forms an element in Nico Muhly's recent opera, *Two Boys*.[36] It can indeed be threatening. 'A [school] bully can reach their target 24/7, victims cannot get away from it.'[37]

The relationship between consumers and celebrities has changed. 'Relations of intimacy are constructed through the media rather than face-to-face meetings. Many people feel a connection with a particular celebrity despite the fact that they have never actually met them.'[38] Achievement-based fame may be replaced by media-driven renown.

Imagined presence

The political scientist, Ben Anderson, notable authority on Indonesia and Thailand, is most famous for his suggestion that nations are 'imagined communities'. It may be that his

---

[33] Ibid., 4/7 January 2011.

[34] Ibid., 3 March 2011.

[35] Quoted in Simon Marginson *et al.*, *International Student Security* (Melbourne: Cambridge University Press, 2010), p.351.

[36] Reviewed by Guy Damann, *Times Literary Supplement*, 29 July 2011, pp.17-18.

[37] Angela Pertusini in *The Daily Telegraph* [UK], 25 June 2011.

[38] John Harris, *Rugby Union and Globalization* (Basingstoke: Palgrave Macmillan, 2010), p.56.

notion has at times been misinterpreted to mean the conception of imagined boundaries. What he meant, at least at first, was, I think, something rather different: our sense of community with members of an entity whom we have never met and never shall meet. 'It is *imagined* because the members of even the smallest nation never know most of their fellow-members, meet them, or even hear of them, yet in the mind of each lives the image of their communion.' Why, he asks, have so many died for 'such limited imaginings'?[39]

The concept recalls Hans Kohn's concept of nationalism: 'our identification with the life and aspirations of uncounted millions whom we shall never know, with a territory which we shall never visit in its entirety.'[40] It is indeed hard to account for the sense of nationality, strong though it is.

Consider the cold-blooded Prosper Mérimée's rabid reaction to Victor Hugo's reference to the motherland as an idea. 'The motherland an idea! It is the image of what is most tangible in the world, it is the flesh of our flesh, the spirit of our spirit, the heart of our heart. It is the living amalgam of our ancestors, of our father, of ourselves; it is the vibration of the voices of us all.'[41]

It may not be, however, what is foremost in a soldier's mind when he finally goes into battle, more, perhaps, committed to the mates whom he knows. Few of the Bavarian regiment in which Hitler served in the first world war were really inspired by the 'spirit of 1914', and they disliked the Prussians as much as the French. '[T]hey were kept going, like all soldiers, by *kameradschaft*, group loyalty.'[42]

---

[39] Benedict Anderson, *Imagined Communities* (London, New York: Verso, 1991), pp.6-7.

[40] Hans Kohn, *The Idea of Nationalism: A Study in Its Origins and Background* (New York: Macmillan, 1944), p.9.

[41] Quoted in A.W. Raitt, *Prosper Mérimée* (London: Eyre and Spottiswoode, 1970), p.315.

[42] Michael Howard, reviewing Thomas Weber, *Hitler's First War*, *Times Literary Supplement*, 11 February 2011.

Evoked presence

Some of the sense of imagined community is, of course, induced by national leaders and nation-makers. Sites of memory are used to evoke a human presence, at some times more genuinely historical than others. Do they overcome what some see as our dwindling sense of history?

Protectors of George Washington's headquarters at Newburg argued in 1850 that 'if our love of country is excited when we read the biography of our revolutionary heroes … how much more will the flame of patriotism burn in our bosoms when we tread the ground where was shed the blood of our fathers, or when we move among the scenes where were conceived and consummated their noble achievements'.[43]

War memorials as a tribute to ordinary soldiers, by distinction from plaques about distinguished individuals on the walls of churches or former dwellings, only began in Britain following the Crimean War of the 1850s.[44] Lutyen's stones of remembrance and Blomfield's cross of sacrifice distinguish British war graves in 140 countries throughout the world. They 'will exist in 2,000 years', Churchill declared, 'and will preserve the memory of a common purpose pursued by a great nation in the remote past and will undoubtedly excite the wonder and reverence of future generations'.[45]

In 1966, urns containing the remains of thousands of civilians killed during the Japanese occupation were entombed in a 200ft-high memorial in Singapore in 1966-7. It was unveiled on the 25th anniversary of the start of the occupation.[46]

'Here (on Stewart Island and in the country as a whole, even allowing for the Maori past), there are no deep layers of human history, no improbably ancient stones. The human presence sits lightly on the natural landscape; the discernible

---

[43] Quoted by Kynan Gentry in Gentry and Gavin McLean (eds), *Heartlands* (Harmondsworth: Penguin, 2006), p.21.

[44] Jock Phillips in Gentry and McLean (eds), *Heartlands.*, p.77.

[45] *The Times*, 11 November 1977.

[46] *The Times*, 2 November 1966, 16 February 1967.

human impact has been slight', John Wilson writes of New Zealand. '... The paradox of historic sites in places like Stewart Island, like New Zealand as a whole, is that a more powerful sense of the past, more vivid connections back to past lives, are attainable here than in places where centuries and centuries of change and destruction have obliterated the traces of many pasts.' He suggests that 'our short past, and the juxtaposition of "wild and won annulled", make us more aware in New Zealand than elsewhere of the fragility of human experience'.[47]

Individually, of course, we have our own such sites. Walking in Trinity College garden, the Cambridge historian G. M. Trevelyan used to think of the great men who had walked there before: 'once, on this earth, once, on this familiar spot of ground, walked other men and women, as actual as we are today, thinking their own thoughts, swayed by their own passions, but now all gone, ... gone as utterly as we ourselves shall shortly be gone like ghost at cockcrow.'[48] Many of us will recall an accurate or inaccurate memory of event or person when visiting a particular site or handling a particular object or seeing a yellowing photo.

In the 1970s my former colleague, the late Dame Judith Binney, trekked through the remote Urewera forest with friends and they came upon a place called Maungapohatu: 'a collection of derelict buildings, few people and a feeling they were intruding.' A shiver had gone up her spine, Dame Judith later recalled. 'She could simply feel the history of that place, she said, that here was a sense of "a very present past".' It was that of the Tuhoe people and the prophet Rua Kenana.[49]

At the close of her book on the piano in colonial New Zealand, Kirstine Moffat called to mind her journeys in the country and in the mind. 'A poignantly delightful moment occurred when I sat on the piano stool in front of the gleaming [1906] Steinway Grand in the drawing room of Olveston House in Dunedin. ... I began to play Franz Liszt's

---

[47] In Gentry and McLean (eds), *Heartlands*, pp.51-2.

[48] G.M. Trevelyan, *An Autobiography and Other Essays* (London, New York: Longmans, 1949), p.13.

[49] *New Zealand Herald*, 17 February 2011.

Consolation 3. The first deep D Flat resonated round the room. The bass arpeggios effortlessly supported the treble melody. Each note rang out, pure and true. The music transported me and connected me, through time, to those who have gone before.'[50]

Mozart was Tchaikovsky's favourite composer. In 1886 he was able to see the autograph score of *Don Giovanni*, kept as a relic by the great singer Pauline Viardot. 'I cannot express the feeling that overcame me when I was looking at this holy musical object – as if I had shaken the hand of Mozart himself and conversed with him.'[51]

Elgar was thrilled in 1908 when Sgambati showed him some of the historic possessions Liszt had left him. 'The first copy of the score *Siegfried Idyll* sent by Wagner to Liszt in Rome with a little writing on the title. Also the *first* exemplar of *Faust* (Berlioz) sent by B. to Liszt! & above all (1868) the full score *Meistersinger* sent by W. to L. with words & the title "*De profundis clamavi!*" at the top, a date etc. below & *Richard*. How wonderful to see and touch.'[52]

In today's celebrity culture fans seek memorabilia in the hope that some of the megastar magic may rub off on them. William Doyle has set up a museum in County Kildare dedicated to cast-offs, including the black cocktail dress Audrey Hepburn wore in *Charade* and the only two garments owned by Grace Kelly that do not belong to the Grace Kelly Foundation. More than 350 000 people visited the Museum in 2010. 'People are fascinated by the fact that these icons actually wore these pieces', Doyle said.[53]

And shall we be remembered? Jean Durourd of the French Academy sought to become immortal through his works. 'To be read by posterity is my kingdom of heaven.' He felt that he

---

[50] Kirstine Moffat, *Piano Forte Stories and Soundscapes from Colonial New Zealand* (Dunedin: University of Otago Press, 2011), p.218.

[51] Quoted in Carolyn Abbate and Roger Parker, *A History of Opera. The Last Four Hundred Years* (London: Allen Lane, 2102), p.138.

[52] Quoted in Kennedy, *Portrait of Elgar*, p.187.

[53] *New Zealand Herald*, 30 March 2011.

was misunderstood by his contemporaries. When he was dead, people 'will see me as I really am'. It was difficult for people to like their neighbours. After death, 'I shall be liked, because I shall no longer be there'.[54]

Absence

Absence is said to make the heart grow fonder. But it is generally associated with sadness. The memory of happy times was a Dantean curse, but perhaps it is a compensation for loss and leave-taking. Maybe it is to be preferred to intrusive presence on the part of counsellors and grief management professionals moving us towards 'closure'. Might we want to remain 'open'? 'The popular idea of "closure" is rubbish, in my view'. Richard Gill writes. '… Closure for me, indicates an end, a finality: it sounds like a politically correct way of shutting the door on painful experience and avoiding reality.'[55]

We have always been influenced in action or inaction by a mixture of the actual and the virtual. The 'presence' of the latter has increased, both in current life and in the recall of the past. Like most human inventions, the e-media can be both misused and well used. There is no substitute for human presence, but the offered substitutes can be powerful, perhaps more powerful than they should be.

---

[54] Quoted in T. Zeldin, *The French* (London: Fontana, 1984), p.345.

[55] Richard Gill, *Give Me Excess of It* (Sydney: Macmillan, 2012), p.267.

5. On Human Complexity

I am not able to tell you why human beings are as they are:
they are, after all, still working on it. Is it because, as the
Greeks thought, they were in Shakespeare's words, the
plaything of the gods? Or did the God of the Old Testament
create them and then they fell, even as they sought
knowledge? Or is it all a matter of chemical reaction or
electrical impulse?

Here we have a species that is wonderfully well endowed,
and whose brain size, I understand, continues to expand, and
it sees itself, though with less certainty than once it did, as
some kind of purposed or final flowering for which the world
itself was created, and which, more certainly, can decide its
fate. It has indeed so many talents, so many attributes: to
employ its mind, to develop its body; to record the past, to
imagine the future; to create and to destroy, to speak and sing,
to work together and apart, to rage, to calm, to hit, to stroke.
'Sure he that made us with such large discourse, Looking
before and after, gave us not that capability and god-like
reason To fust in us unus'ed.'[1] The species can feel and express
shame and anxiety, inhibition and insecurity, happiness and
despair. It can love and hate and kill and end its own life. And
as you will note it can go on.

It is indeed what John Locke would have defined as a
complex: an Idea 'made up of several simple ones put
together'; his examples indeed included Beauty, Gratitude, the
Army and also 'Man', by which he meant humankind.
Complexity, a word first used in 1721, was of course the
quality or condition of being complex.

That complexity conduces to diversity. Even though we
are physically complicated in almost entirely similar ways, we
are all different. Rachel Joyce's Harold finds he 'could no
longer pass a stranger without acknowledging the truth that
everyone was the same, and also unique, and that this was the

---

[1] *Hamlet*, IV, 4, l. 36-9

dilemma of being human'.[2] And we act differently, responding to situations in different ways, each of us subject, for example, to varying levels of road rage or tempted in varying degrees to red-light running, whatever the level of the alcoholic intake to which we have been tempted for whatever range of reasons.

Working on a book on Vietnam, I came across John Connally's appraisal of President Johnson: 'He was cruel and kind, generous and greedy, crafty and naïve, ruthless and thoughtful, simple in many ways and yet extremely complex, caring and totally not caring. ... it would take every adjective in the dictionary to describe him.'[3]

And of course over longer periods each of us (like Rachel Joyce's Harold) changes, partly because we are not fabricated to last forever, and the whole complexus can come to seem rather Heath Robinson as the switches appear to turn themselves off one by one, if not all at once, and you move to the point, Shakespeare again, of 'second childishness and mere oblivion, sans teeth, sans eyes, sans taste, sans everything'.[4] The first attribute to go is memory, though I did not need Ben Jonson – [was it?] to remind me. 'Memory, of all powers of the mind, is the most delicate and frail; it is the first of our faculties that age invades.'[5]

We are constituted not only by our nature but by our nurture and cannot consider how the individual acts in reference only the possession of human common attributes. How we behave depends on circumstances and on the passage of time, but also on our relationship with other human beings, past and present. Even those who take vows of silence have acknowledged the existence of a human community, though deciding that they will be better off, at least in some respects, without it. [Stylites?] And people involuntarily separated from society have included some who

---

[2] Rachel Joyce, *The Unlikely Pilgrimage of Harold Fry* (London: Black Swan, 2013), pp.180-1.

[3] Quoted in Mark K. Updegrove, *Indomitable Will LBJ in the Presidency* (New York: Crown, 2102), p.3]

[4] Jaques, in *As You Like It*, 7, 2. 164-5

[5] Quoted in Ian Donaldson, *Ben Jonson A Life* (Oxford University Press, 2011), p.14.

have thought about it most deeply. A period of colonial imprisonment used sometimes to be regarded as a qualification for leading an independent nation. Not everyone emerged from imprisonment with so much to say of importance to others as Primo Levi, Nehru, Solzhenitsyn and Nelson Mandela. And I suppose not many have been so damaged by the society they were brought up in as Stalin. 'He was a typical Goreli', Simon Sebag Montefiore tells us, 'for the denizen of Gori was notorious throughout Georgia as a *matrabazi*, a boastful violent scallywag. Gori was one of the last towns to practise the "picturesque and savage" custom of free-for-all town brawls with special rules but no holds barred violence. … The saloon bars of Gori were incorrigible stews of violence and crime.'[6]

That had derived from the legacy of medieval Georgia when, as an independent state, it was continually at war. And of course, the social context of the individual's action changes over time as do other circumstances. What, for example, seems entirely acceptable in one society may be deemed an individual eccentricity in another, and people will shape their behaviour by accepting instruction or internalising practice. My example takes me to the British Raj of Sarawak. The founding Raja, James Brooke, surrounded himself with very young men, often midshipmen on the naval vessels whose aid he sought. Was it a homosexual relationship? modern historians have asked. Was it active? they may go on. I doubt if these are legitimate questions and whether they are answerable. In the 1830s and 1840s, the relationships among males were spoken of in terms that differ from those we use. Something similar may be said of the two men in Bizet's opera *The Pearl-fishers*, composed in the early 1860s. In the famous duet Nadir and Zurga [Zenith Shaw wanted to call him] sing of their love for another, committing themselves to avoid competing for the lovely Leila. A Sydney production turned it round. Leila has come between Zurga and Nadir: Nadir is her rival. Just the kind of opera production I detest. I am

---

[6] Simon Sebag Montefiore, *Young Stalin* (London: Phoenix, 2007), p.35.

interested in the opera and what its creators meant, not what a producer imposes a century and a half later.

Given human complexity and diversity, human societies are sure to be diverse. What does the individual seek? That kind of question is one political philosophers have sought to answer, Locke among them. For many there is no choice, though such philosophers may base their theory on the notion that there is. Others offer a qualified acceptance and want improvement. The primary aim is surely security. What we can achieve without that is limited, and our lives may be in Hobbesian phrase nasty, brutish and short. Nowadays we expect security to be provided by the state, indeed Hobbes was writing of Leviathan, though of course it has been sought in other ways, especially when the state is weak or uninterested. In early Poland, as elsewhere, you looked to a lord, whose service you might enter, and who would as a result owe you protection. The reciprocity model exists in other societies, and indeed it survives in some degree within modern states, though words like nepotism and corruption may also be applied. Where the state was not interested, human beings might seek strength among their fellows through association. The pang societies of Chinese migrants to nineteenth-century Malaya and Singapore are an instance. Mostly male, they left their districts in southern China to make some money in the Straits and remit it home before themselves returning, as they hoped. The colonial government left them to it, intervening very little before the 1880s. You joined for protection, for welfare, to make sure of a proper burial if you did not live to return.

These examples suggest the compromise involved: your freedom is limited at the very same time as it is preserved. And, of course, there is a risk that you will not secure the protection you seek. Your protector or your association may feel obliged to struggle with another: your life may be put at risk by conflict created by the ambitions or interests [or hubris?] of the protectors or their opponents. And even they may be disappointed. Outcomes are seldom predictable, and people may in any case act out of miscalculation or desperation.

Georges Bernanos, the French author, was impatient with all human institutions. He wrote of the spirit of France and its contribution to civilisation. But Frenchmen of his own day let him down: he wanted too much from them. 'The [Great] war has left me dumbfounded, like everyone else, by the vast disproportion between the enormity of the *sacrifice* and the wretched ideology proposed to us by the governments and the press.'[7] Important though his experience of the war was for him, the feeling it aroused in him was only an extreme version of what he felt about other human institutions. He was almost permanently angry: he expressed his anger in words, he expressed it in an animal laughter peculiarly his. The Spanish Civil War prompted disgust with the right-wing: 'crimes committed in the name of religion', he indeed concluded, 'were more reprehensible than those committed against it.'[8] Out of the defeat of France he hoped for something better, but the *épuration* again disappointed him. There was no rebirth, only an 'atrocious truth', as André Rousseaux put it. 'The reality of contemporary France, which no genuine victory had effaced, was the capitulation of 1940. That is why, on the day when Paris was liberated, Bernanos remained silent.'[9]

It is perhaps in some of the creative arts that we find these tensions best expressed. Societies and governments have not always allowed that, though their intervention has prompted some of the most heartfelt and most profound attempts to do so, often through indirect language or symbolism or music such as that of Shostakovich. But politicians have spoken well on the subject, if not always acted well, or been able to act well. In a speech he made in 1961 at St Joseph's Institution, a secondary school in Singapore, David Marshall, a fine lawyer who had briefly been prime minister in the 1950s, put it like this: 'Because human beings live together, they find in mutual co-operation far greater opportunities for the expression of individual personality, and it is because of the consequent

---

[7] Quoted in Robert Speaight, *Georges Bernanos* (London: Harvill, 1973), pp.61, 69.

[8] Ibid., p.171.

[9] ibid., pp.244-5.

need to maintain peaceful co-operation between individuals who form a society that groups of human beings, since the earliest history of man, have enforced group discipline. Such group discipline should never be so rigid as to exclude originality which extends beyond the boundary of human experience even though seemingly anti-social but should be adequate to act as deterrent to conduct, affecting the security and comfort of the people as a whole.'[10] It is the issue Reuel Lochore raised in New Zealand. 'Who are we? What are we? Why are we here? How could communities better organise themselves to empower individuals to lead more fulfilling lives?'[11]

If a society can help and, or threaten an individual, it may also threaten or help other societies. We are all human, but not organised in one society, but in many, and in diverse and often complex ways. Societies may be sustained by ritual, practice and habit, by regulation, by ideology. A feature is their distinctness from other societies. One aid to organising a society is indeed to stress its difference from other societies, to make a society unique even though it is composed of creatures that are in so many respects so similar. Tensions result, intended or not. Cohesion is bought at the risk of conflict.

'Most of us define ourselves', says the cynical boss in Carlos Ruiz Zafón's novel *The Angel's Game*, 'by opposing rather than favouring something or someone. …. It is easier to react than to act. Nothing arouses a passion for dogma more than a good antagonist.' It is difficult to have an idea, he continues. 'It's much easier to hate someone with a recognisable face whom we can blame for everything that makes us feel uncomfortable. It doesn't have to be an individual character. It can be a nation, a race, a group. … anything.'[12]

---

[10] Quoted in Chan Heng Chee, *A Sensation of Independence* (Singapore: Oxford University Press, 1984), p.8.

[11] Quoted in Michael King, *Tread Softly* (Auckland: Cape Catley, 2001), p.66.

[12] Carlos Ruiz Zafón, *The Angel's Game* (London: Phoenix, 2010), p.285.

Only a super-computer designed by IBM could beat Gasparov at chess. What are the limits of human intelligence? We cannot tell. One of the characteristics of human complexity, however, seems to be a desire for simplicity: is it a necessary counterpart? Interestingly the word carries overtones both of honesty and stupidity. Our personalities, our relationships with others, our past, present and future, offer challenges that are indeed complex. It is not surprising that we look for an answer to our questions, and that we may be ready to seek it by simplification, to blame a person or a people, or find, too readily, too thoughtlessly, a 'basic', sometimes a 'most basic', explanation. And if human complexity is further complicated by the organization of societies that provide individuals at a price with the security they need, and that themselves, like individuals though in a different way, change over time, it is not surprising that they resort to stereotyping.

Perhaps stereotyping is a characteristic reaction to an initial encounter with the strange, with the Other. Stereotyping, Sander Gilman suggests, is a 'universal means of coping with anxieties engendered by our inability to control the world'.[13] In the Ancient world, the barbarians were an undifferentiated mass that lay outside the bounds of civilisation. For the Chinese emperors, something similar was true, though others might have a place in the world by the acknowledgment of their tributary status. But we need not look so far back. The globalisation that began in the sixteenth century and has continued has involved continual encounters with unfamiliar societies. The initial reaction may be to stereotype, and it may be to the interest of leaders to encourage it. Kaiser Wilhelm infamously invoked the Yellow Peril [while at the same time proclaiming his readiness to protect Islam]. And he was not, of course, alone. Sir George Grey had used the phrase in New Zealand, even when

---

[13] Sander Gilman, *Difference and Pathology: Stereotypes of Sexuality, Race and Madness* (Ithaca: Cornell University Press, 1985), p.12.

Chinese formed but 1.9% of the population.[14] There were other stereotypes, too, including those built on the migration of the Jews into Western Europe who sought to escape the pogroms in the East.

Yet, of course, German scholars were the closest students of the Bible, though not of the Chinese classics. Contacts between regions have been both peaceful and violent. Indeed the two modes have been mixed. Conquerors have been attracted by the wealth and civilisation of their neighbours. When successful, they have assimilated as much as imposed, if not more: 'hybridity' is a word that has been utilised. An older narrative pictured a conflict between migrant tribes and sedentary populations, in which the winner took all, as Norman Davies puts it. Now it is realised that migrations 'did not necessarily involve wholesale expulsions or mass slaughter; more usually, they caused a high degree of ethnic mixing and cultural assimilation between the incomers and their predecessors'.[15] Sometimes, like the 13th-century Mongols of Genghis Khan and his successors, they opened, at the price of initial bloodshed and destruction, new links between regions and extended the opportunity for trade and other contacts. The conflict between the Muslims and the Crusaders did not interdict, far from it, the borrowings Christian Europe made from Arab culture, which had itself been enriched by Indian culture as well as Greek.

Samuel Huntington posited a conflict of 'civilisations', an even more generalised lumping of potential or actual antagonists. Contrast Felipe Fernández-Armesto. 'Even when locked in what appears to be mutual hostility, like Ancient Rome and Persia, or medieval Christendom and Islam, civilizations tend to develop relationships which are mutually acknowledging and mutually sustaining. ... Though there are occasional exceptions, it seems hard for any civilization to

---

[14] Nicholas Tarling, *New Zealand The Making of an Asia-Pacific Society* (Auckland: Confucius Institute, 2011), p.39.

[15] Norman Davies, *Vanished Kingdoms* (Harmondsworth: Penguin, 2011), p.240.

survive at a high level of material achievement, except in contact with others.'[16]

Edward Said's widely read *Orientalism* is open to criticism for itself doing what it criticised, stereotyping, essentializing. 'Said's rhetorical representation of Orientalism as a unified discourse buys into the very logic it opposes', Varisco writes. 'By building his counter-argument on the same fundamental distinction between two essentialized abstractions, Said does little more than replace one flawed scheme with another.'[17] He 'occidentalizes' the West by 'essentializing' 'the characteristics of European powers', suggests John Mackenzie.[18]

Indeed, in *Musical Elaborations*, Said seems to consider that the West had essentialized itself as well as the East. 'For in the encounter between the West and its various "Others" (to employ a fashionable, but still useful word) there was often a tactic of drawing a defensive perimeter called "the West" around anything done by individual nations or persons who concentrated a self-appointed Western essence in themselves; this tactic protected against change and a supposed contamination brought forward threateningly by the very existence of the Other. In addition, such defensiveness permits a comforting retreat into an essentialized, basically unchanging Self. By the same token, there is a move to freeze the Other in a kind of basic objecthood.'[19]

Two years later, in *Culture and Imperialism* [1993], Said indeed accepted that the relationship of East and West was more subtle, more complicated, than he had earlier argued: there were more interaction, more borrowing, more cultural exchange. Only a perspective 'contrapuntal and often nomadic' was 'fully sensitive to the reality of historical

---

[16] F. Fernández-Armesto, *Civilisations: Culture, Ambition and the Transformation of Nature* (New York: Free Press, 2001), pp.25-6.

[17] Ibid., p.49.

[18] John M. Mackenzie, *Orientalism History, Theory and the Arts* (Manchester: Manchester University Press, 1995), p.5.

[19] Edward W. Said, *Musical Elaborations* (New York: Columbia University Press, 1991), p.52.

experience. Partly because of empire, all cultures are involved in one another; none is single and pure, all are hybrid, heterogenous, extraordinarily differentiated, and unmonolithic'.[20]

'Conversations across boundaries can be fraught', says Kwame Anthony Appiah, 'all the more so as the world grows smaller, and the stakes grow larger. It's therefore worth remembering that they can also be a pleasure. ... The way of segregation and seclusion has always been anomalous in our perpetually voyaging species. Cosmopolitanism isn't hard work; repudiating it is.'[21]

Indeed, it might be that our complexity is asserting itself: curiosity competes with ignorance; a wish to make contact with reticence and antagonism. Or if contact is established, a community may be unwilling to disturb it, even though it contains inequalities of wealth or power. Sometimes a leader will have to work hard to stir up antagonism, so as to justify or enhance his position and what he intends to do. Mao comes to mind.

Village life in China before the communist conquest was extraordinarily diverse, especially in the south. 'Nowhere in this profusion of social diversity could anybody called a "landlord" (*dizhu*) be found. ... It had no meaning for most people in the countryside, who referred to some of their more fortunate neighbours as *caizhu*, an appellation that implied prosperity yet carried no derogatory undertones.' Absent landowners abused their power, malpractices were rife, but there was no dominant class of *Junkers* or squires, no equivalent of serfdom, no 'feudalism'.[22] Mao's land reform of 1947-8, so called, had to take another form. 'Everywhere work teams dug up old grudges, fanned resentment and turned local grievances into class hatred, and everywhere mobs were worked into a frenzy of envy as they appropriated the

---

[20] Edward W. Said, *Culture and Imperialism* (New York, Columbia University Press, 1993), p.xxiv.

[21] Kwame Anthony Appiah, *Cosmopolitanism: Ethics in a World of Strangers* (New York: Norton, 2006), p.xx.

[22] Frank Dikotter, *The Tragedy of Liberation* (New York: Bloomsbury, 2013), p.70.

possessions of traditional village leaders.'[23] In some places it got out of hand. In Hebei, Liu Shaoqi reported, 'when the masses fight, they beat, torture and kill people'.[24]

That was in the midst of civil war. But what happened in the south from 1950 was, though Stalin himself urged moderation, not dissimilar. 'Mao wanted the traditional village leaders overthrown so that nothing would stand between the people and the party. ... And unlike the Soviet Union, where the security organs had liquidated the kulaks, Mao wanted the farmers to do the job themselves. The moral values and social bonds of reciprocity that had long regulated village life were to be destroyed by pitting a majority against a minority. Only by implicating the people in murder could they become permanently linked to the party. ... Everyone was to have blood on their hands through participation in mass rallies and denunciation meetings.'[25] [cf Suharto] Majority and minority were thus created. Stereotypes imposed. And the restraints on greed and envy [and dobbing in] removed.

In other societies differences were at hand, though they also had to be worked on. So-called 'race' was one, as the Kaiser and his successor recognised. And that was more easily done if skin colour differed, utterly superficial distinction though it was. 'Complexion' indeed is etymologically related to 'complexity'. Initially the word alluded to the combination of an individual's qualities, his or her 'humours' or emphasis among humankind's 'four temperaments'. Then it came to describe the colour and texture of the skin, originally as showing temperament: and that element is still there, so that the ruddy-complexioned look jolly and kindly, and the sallow somewhat sinister. Skin colour dislodged the notion without quite eliminating it. Blacks were inferior, yellow, too, but more of a threat. Browns might be 'little brown brothers', like the Filipinos, extinguishable like the Tasmanians, rather formidable, though doomed, like the Maori. One inadequate science replaced another, to even more dangerous effect.

---

[23] Ibid., p.74.
[24] Quoted in ibid., p.73.
[25] Ibid., pp.75-6.

Nowadays we avoid talking. rightly, of 'race'. But we attach people to their 'ethnicity' or their 'culture', again stereotyping at grave risk to an understanding of their complex individuality, even while purposing protection and support; risking, too, ignoring change. Perhaps, too, it risks the stability of the complex society in which they live and with which they have a reciprocal relationship. Even, it may be, there is a risk to the larger human society which globalisation has created, though we seem more or less ready to accept the dual allegiances of diaspora and the implications of transmigration. Why do we engage in this categorisation? Sometimes, it seems, just because we can.

Taking a census was part of making a state from early times. The nineteenth-twentieth century colonial state insisted on including 'racial' and 'tribal' affiliations. 'There is no doubt', a North Borneo census report remarked in 1931, 'that a good deal of confusion and doubt exists not only in the minds of the enumerators but of the natives themselves as to which [tribal] subdivision they really belong in.'[26] The people had identified themselves with the rivers along which they lived and through which they communicated with others. Now they had to decide their identity on another basis, or internalise one thrust upon them.

Census-takers remain obsessed with identity, even, or especially, in the post-modern nation state. In recent New Zealand censuses we have been successively asked with which 'ethnic group' we 'identify' or 'belong to', and offered a weird mix of possible answers. 'Information on the communities that make up our country', the Statistics Minister has explained, was 'key' to making New Zealand prosper. So we learn that one in three of those who 'identified with the Manx ethnic group' speak Maori and 53.1% say they have never smoked regularly. The census was a 'fantastic tool', said Henry Chung, Associate Professor of Marketing at Massey University. 'The reality is the needs and demands for goods and services are very different for each ethnic community.' For example, moon-cakes were a must-have product for the

---

[26] Quoted in M. Clark Roff, *The Politics of Belonging* (Kuala Lumpur: Oxford University Press, 1974), p.207.

Chinese community for the Moon Festival. The data would help the Pak'n Save chain 'identify the supermarkets where the demand for mooncakes would be highest'.[27] One must presume that the Manx would not eat them. Anyway only 108 New Zealanders 'identified' as Manx or 'belonged to' that 'ethnic group'.

In the US census of 1940 'Hindu' appeared as a race category; in 1970 Indian and Pakistani Americans were declared to be 'white'; in 1980 'Asian'. In 2000 respondents were asked to describe themselves as belonging to one or more of 15 'racial' identities': if they refused, their racial identity would be imputed by the Census Bureau.[28] I leave the 'ethnicity' answer on my New Zealand census form blank, and I suppose something similar happens. The fact is that, like others, I 'identify' with much and 'belong to' none. Maybe I would put 'historian' first. Or grumpy old man.

The questions and the posited answers would be ludicrous if they were not dangerous. David Cannadine has pointed to the risks of what has been termed 'totalising', 'namely the habit of describing and defining individuals by their membership in one single group, deemed to be more important and more all-encompassing than any other solidarity, and indeed than all others, to which they might simultaneously belong'. He quotes the criticism the African American feminist Bernice Reagon offered of Germaine Greer's 'totalising'. 'Every time you see a woman you're looking at a human being who is like you in only one respect, but may be totally different from you in three or four others.'[29]

The other much used word is 'culture'. That, of course, has shifted its meaning over time. Currently it is often used as a label of difference alongside 'identity', rather paradoxical though that they may be. It carries overtones of the stereotyping that arises from the alien or unfamiliar. 'How should we do business with people from other cultures?' a recent 'Asia Savvy' conference held at NZAI was asked. Of

---

[27] *New Zealand Herald*, 20 August 2014.

[28] David Cannadine, *The Undivided Past* (Harmondsworth: Penguin, 2013), p.217.

[29] Ibid., p.152.

course, in foreign countries, they do things differently, as they did in the past. But human beings are more complex than that suggests, and they change in changing circumstances.

Remember that census is organised on a national basis and Asia Savvy was held at a New Zealand university. The nation-state, created in the 19th and 20th centuries, still calls for our primary allegiance in return for its endeavour to provide security and welfare. But remember, too, that the nation-state is itself, in Benedict Anderson's famous formulation, an 'imagined community'. We may identify with it or belong to it, though the New Zealand census did not encourage us to say so. But it is an extraordinary 'community', since most of its members are unknown to us. We are identifying with people we have never met, with whom we have little else in common, indeed whose complexity ensures a diversity of interests and objectives. And for such an abstraction, a 'limited imagining', as Ben Anderson calls it, people have given their lives.

My [muddled] disquisition has focused on complexity, individual and social, through a counterpart, simplicity, not in the sense of limpidity or dimwittedness, but rather in the sense of simplification. Stereotyping the relationship with others is a way of facing the problems that complexity raises, a risky one, perhaps, even a dangerous one. And maybe too easy. Part of human complexity is a desire to order, to find order or make it. Another part is to emulate or imitate, to adopt fashions, hideous or otherwise, even to accept the imposed as your own, as with the Chinese pigtail, to mark difference and assert individuality [where can't you pierce your body or tattoo it?]. Yet another: to envy, and so to turn on neighbours, or anonymously to dob in, or join in a riot. And there are pleasures to be found, so I understand, in other ways of abandoning complexity, taking drugs or dancing with 'abandon' or meditating and 'emptying your mind'.

We do get together to understand and analyse complexity, to pool intelligence. Often we are pushed together by the need for security, the pressures of society, the state, for weapons research most obviously, or by the prospect of funding and economic survival. But not always: sheer zest for understanding, sheer lust for knowing, to adapt the title of Robert Irwin's book, is surely part of human complexity.

Simplification is, of course, a word OED recognises. I do not find complexification, and I hope I have not invented a need for it. Identifying myself as a historian, I would like to think I have not abandoned the wide prospect that W.H. McNeill opened for the profession by his advocacy of world history. 'Humanity entire possesses a commonality which historians may hope to understand just as firmly as they can comprehend what unites any lesser group. Instead of enhancing conflicts, as parochial historiography inevitably does, an intelligible world history might be expected to diminish the lethality of group encounters by cultivating a sense of individual identification with the triumphs and tribulations of humanity as a whole.'[30]

Gustav Holst quoted Thomas Hardy in his score *Egdon Heath*. May I quote it in conclusion? 'A place perfectly accordant with man's nature – neither ghastly, hateful, nor ugly; neither commonplace, unmeaning, nor tame; but, like man, slighted and enduring; and withal singularly colossal and mysterious in its swarthy monotony.'

---

[30] Quoted ibid., pp.263-4.

6. On Judgment

Judgment is a human quality, although, in one sense, it is shared with other creatures. Indeed, a bird landing on a branch may be making a rather better judgment of space/time than the driver who overtakes me at the wrong moment on the motorway. But today I speak as an historian, not an endangered motorist or a one-time amateur ornithologist, and an historian exercises judgment in a different way and in general on a different topic, the actions of human beings in the circumstances in which they have acted. Historians, mostly human I believe, have certainly made such judgments, and indeed 'History' is expected to do so. But can they? can it?. Or should that be a matter for the courts? Or of Divine justice?

The past can certainly be used to make judgments about the present, and the present can impose its judgments on the past. Sometimes it is a matter of praise and condemnation: his was a worthy example; he, though a worthy man, mistook the trend of history, a Strafford, for example, working for a 'lost cause'. This or that was 'the verdict of history'. In his famous book, *The Whig Interpretation of History*, Herbert Butterfield was especially concerned over text-books that worked by abridgment: putting people on one side or other in the making of the national story made it easier to tell and implicitly involved a kind of judgment, if not explicitly, Sellars and Yeatman style: King John was a bad king. But if seeking examples, or looking for justification, are not satisfactory ways of relating past and present, must that relationship exclude all attempts at judgment?

An element of judgment is indeed involved in the type of analysis that attempts to determine the causes of a war or a revolution, and perhaps to ascertain the role of an individual in such a crisis. May the historian take the further step of commenting on that role? exercising judgement about an individual's judgment? The importance of the individual's action may be assessed. But to offer a judgment as to its being 'reasonable' or 'appropriate', our current word for 'good', is a more doubtful venture, since it may presume more knowledge of the individual's motivation than the historian has or perhaps can possibly have, and since in any case it increases the risk of importing the historian's present into the past. 'Very often the knave and the hero are distinguished less by their action than by their motivation', Henry Kissinger observed.[1] But the individual cannot be interviewed or cross-examined or water-boarded; and the historian cannot get so far into their minds, whether or not they have left diaries or letters.

It may still, however, be possible to comment on the quality or nature of a particular decision, and consider its outcome. The historian is, for example, probably able to say whether in 1914 the Kaiser and his government decided on war, stumbled into war, or gambled on avoiding war. That is the kind of judgment he or she may find it possible to make. Is it possible to go further? Some indeed wanted, as the second world war provided, judicial tribunals, others simply to hang the Kaiser. The first was not done, so there were no cross-examinations, and the second, not done either, would have precluded them.

Lord Acton wanted to judge 'great men' of the past, such as the pre-Reformation Popes by the standards of Victorian law. 'Historic responsibility has to make up for the want of legal responsibility.' Hence his 1887 dictum that power tended to corrupt, and absolute power corrupted absolutely. His correspondent, historian and Bishop Mandell Creighton, questioned that. 'Selfishness, even wrong doing, for an idea, an institution, the maintenance of an accepted view, does not cease to be wrongdoing: but it is not quite the same as personal wrongdoing. ... The men who conscientiously thought heresy a crime may be accused of an intellectual mistake, not necessarily of a moral crime ... I am hopelessly tempted to admit degrees of criminality. ... the actors were men like myself, sorely tempted by the possession of power, trammelled by holding a representative position, ... and in the sixteenth century especially looking at things in a very abstract way. ... I cannot follow the actions of contemporary

---

[1] Quoted in Niall Ferguson, *Kissinger, 1923-1968: The Idealist* (London: Allen Lane, 2015), p.868.

statesmen with much moral satisfaction. In the past I find myself regarding them with pity. Who am I that I should condemn them?'[2]

The difficulty in making judgments about men, but also the possibility of making judgments about the quality of a particular judgment, arises out of a relationship between past and present that has ineluctably faced the historian ever since Leopold von Ranke. In the preface to his *Histories of the Latin and Teutonic Nations* [1824] he wrote: 'To history has been assigned the task of judging the past, of instructing the world of today for the benefit of future years. The present attempt does not claim such an exalted function; it merely wants to state what actually happened [*er will bloss sagen, wie es eigentlich gewesen*]'. 'Strict description of the fact, although it might limit us and prove to be unpleasant, is without doubt the supreme law.'[3]

It is perhaps no paradox that these words have been almost as often debated as they have been quoted. The pursuit of 'facts' it endorsed tended to be seen as sufficient by some American historians: for them Ranke was 'empirical science incarnate'.[4] 'If one must choose between a school of history whose main characteristic is *esprit*, and one which rests upon a faithful and honest effort to base its whole narration upon the greatest attainable number of recorded facts, we cannot long hesitate,' Ephraim Emerton declared in 1886. '... Training has taken the place of brilliancy and the whole civilized world is today reaping the benefit.'[5] What could be achieved was certainly exaggerated, even by so clearly a brilliant man as Lord Acton: 'all information is within reach, and every problem has become capable of solution.'[6] A more

---

[2] Quoted in ibid., p.877.

[3] Quoted in Felix Gilbert, *History: Politics or Culture. Reflections on Ranke and Burckhardt* (Princeton: Princeton University Press, 1990), p.19.

[4] Quoted in Peter Novick, *That Noble Dream* (Cambridge: Cambridge University Press, 1988), p.28.

[5] Quoted ibid., p.29.

[6] Quoted in G. Himmelfarb, *Lord Acton* (Chicago: Chicago University Press, 1962), p.223.

doubtful age, though one with more information at its disposal, is less confident. Even if 'fact' can be distinguished from 'representation', we still have to select and to construct. (I am not sympathetic to the use of all these quote marks)

Ranke himself did not rule out intuition. 'It is our task to recognize what really [*eigentlich*] happened in the series of facts which German history comprises: their sum. After the labour of criticism, intuition is required.'[7] The meaning of *eigentlich* has shifted since he wrote, when it could mean, not merely 'really' or 'actually', but also 'essentially'. 'Essentially' and perhaps 'really' seem, as Gilbert puts it, 'to refer to a truth that lies beneath the surface of facts; the historian must penetrate this surface to get at the essence of events'. Translating *eigentlich* as 'actually' suggests by contrast 'that the final aim of the historian is the precise rendering of facts'. Gilbert asks what Ranke really meant. His conclusion is that Ranke saw history as a part of literature. 'Showing the past as it had actually been meant not only establishing the facts as correctly as possible, but also placing them in their contemporary context in such a way that the past would come to life again.'[8]

The notion that history should establish this kind of historicist relationship between the present and the past was widely shared. 'The main task of the historian became to find out why people acted as they did by stepping into their shoes, by seeing the world through their eyes and as far as possible judging it by their standards', as John Tosh puts it.[9] History, Thomas Carlyle said, was 'an address (literally out of Heaven, for did not God order it all?) to our *whole* inner man'. He insisted that 'the first indispensable condition' was that 'we *see* the things transacted, picture them wholly as if they stand before our eyes.'[10] 'We do call the past, *as such,* into being by recollecting and by thinking historically; but we do this by

---

[7] Quoted in Novick, *That Noble Dream* , p.28.

[8] Gilbert, *History: Politics or Culture. Reflections on Ranke and Burckhardt* , pp.34, 37.

[9] John Tosh, *The Pursuit of History* (London, New York: Longmans, 1984), p.14.

[10] Quoted in J.R. Hale, *The Evolution of British Historiography* (London: Macmillan, 1967), p.42.

disentangling it out of the present in which it actually exists', R.G. Collingwood thought.[11] But is that disentangling really possible and, if so, how far can it go?

J. A .Froude thought Carlyle's condition could not be met. 'In the alteration of our own character, we have lost the key which would interpret the characters of our fathers, and the great men even of our own English history before the Reformation seem to us almost like the fossil skeletons of another order of beings   Now all is gone; and between us and the old English there lies a gulf of mystery which the prose of the historian will never adequately bridge. They cannot come to us, and our imagination can but feebly penetrate to them.'[12] A century later G.M. Trevelyan repeated the doubt. Much affected by a sense of place, he was affected, too, by a sense of the irretrievable: 'once, on this earth, once, on this familiar spot of ground [Trinity Garden], walked other men and women, as actual as we are today, thinking their own thoughts, swayed by their own passions, but now all gone, ... gone as utterly as we ourselves shall shortly be gone like ghost at cockcrow.'[13]

The only way you could hope to live a dramatic role, Konstantin Stanislavsky believed, was by recreating its inner life, experiencing feelings analogous to it, each time you played it.[14] The actor needed a mind well stocked with actual and artistic experiences, so that he or she could call on the 'emotion-memory' and find something to facilitate imagining the role in hand. The imagination could be exercised so that the actor could better identify with the part.

The historian's task may in some respects be similar. Butterfield seemed to think so: 'historical students must be like actors, who must not merely masquerade as Hamlet on one night and King Lear on another night, but must feel and

---

[11] Quoted in David Lowenthal, *The Past is a Foreign Country* (Cambridge: Cambridge University Press, 1985), p.186.

[12] Quoted in ibid., p.233.

[13] G. M. Trevelyan, *Autobiography and other Essays* (London and New York: Longmans, 1949), p.13.

[14] K. Stanislavsky, *An Actor Prepares,* trans. E.R. Hapgood (London: Bles, 1937), pp.14-15.

think so, and really get under their skins. The defective historian being like the defective actor who does not really dramatize anything, because, in whatever role he is cast, he is always the same: he can only be himself.'[15]

That can in a sense be done. Shakespeare has laid down the text, though of course it can be delivered in various ways, and interpretations are bound to differ. But historians themselves have no ready-made text, and nor in my view can they lay one down with such certainty that they can recreate an inner life or get under the skins of their subject. Without that their judgments will remain limited.

Froude preferred to compare his colleagues to playwrights. 'History is the account of the actions of men, and in "actions" are comprehended the thoughts, opinions, motives, impulses of the actors and of the circumstances in which their work was executed If *Hamlet* or *Lear* was exact to outward fact, were they and their fellow-actors on the stage exactly such as Shakespeare describes them, that was perfect history; and what we call history is only valuable as it approaches to that pattern. To say that the characters of men cannot be thus completely known, that their inner nature is beyond our reach, that the dramatic portraiture of things is only possible to poetry, is to say that history ought not to be written, for the inner nature of the persons of whom it speaks is the essential thing about them.'[16]

The playwright, as Froude recognised, has the world under better control than the historian. As he put it in writing of the historian's duty: 'to penetrate really into the hearts and souls of men, to give each his due, to represent him as he appeared at his best, to himself and not to his enemies, to sympathize in the collision of principles with each party in turn; to feel as they felt, to think as they thought, and to reproduce the various beliefs, the acquirements, the intellectual atmosphere of another age, is a task which requires gifts as great or greater than those of the greatest dramatists; for all is required which

---

[15] H. Butterfield, *History and Human Relations* (London: Collins, 1951), p.248.

[16] J.A. Froude, *Thomas Carlyle* (London: Longmans, 1882-4), II, pp.200-01.

is required of the dramatist, with the obligation to truth of ascertained fact besides.'[17]

I am not sure it can be done. Not by historians anyway: the inner mind is a matter of guess-work, informed or otherwise. What can we really know of our subjects, however elaborate our sources are? '"Never trust biographies", wrote Anne Michaels in her novel *Fugitive Pieces*. "Too many events in a man's life are invisible. Unknown to others as our dreams. And nothing releases the dreamer."'[18] Even elaborate sources will not give us the whole truth and nothing but the truth. Historians also attempt biography, but those who have done so realise that they are engaged in a somewhat different enterprise. One risk, of course, is that it becomes hagiography, a justificatory piece, like an autobiography, a necessarily favourable judgment. Another, particularly in more recent times, is that becomes the reverse, an exercise in debunking of the kind that Lytton Strachey practised so effectively, and others have less elegantly followed.

Biographers have also been tempted in modern times to apply psycho-analysis to figures of the past. Yet the risk of anachronism is surely too great. The popularity of biography has, however, exposed authors to another temptation, not unrelated. Modern readers, perhaps because of the concerns of current society, are curious about the relationship of the public and the private, and reverse the preoccupations of the Victorian 'life and times' biography. The author may thus downplay the engagement of the subject in the issues of the day, and focus on the supposed relationship with the issues of our day. Was Sir James Brooke, Raja of nineteenth-century Sarawak, a homosexual? If so, was he an active one? These are issues that cannot be intelligibly answered, or even perhaps asked.[19]

Both historian and historical novelist are concerned with the past and indeed with the facts. The best historical novelists

---

[17] Ibid., p.201,

[18] Paul Roberts, *Debussy* (London: Phaidon, 2008), p.10.

[19] J.H. Walker has made the attempt. See ' "This peculiar acuteness of feeling": James Brooke and the enactment of desire', in *Borneo Research Bulletin,* 29 (1998), pp.150-89.

at least, set aside those engaged in sensation on the one hand and propaganda on the other, will not tell a deliberate untruth. 'I have never ... in any historical book of mine, falsified anything deliberately which I knew or believed to be true', wrote Mary Renault. 'Often of course I must have done through ignorance what would horrify me if I could revisit the past. ... But one can at least desire the truth; and it is inconceivable to me how anyone can decide deliberately to betray it; to alter some fact which was central to the life of a real human being, however long it is since he ceased to live, in order to make a smoother story, or to exploit him as propaganda for some cause.'[20] Not to falsify is, of course, a requirement on the historian, too. But, unlike the historical novelist, the historian must not invent either. The novelist may, indeed must, though the result should be the product of an historical imagination, and not mere fancy.

Indeed, the novelist has a total design in mind, and not merely a period or a problem. Though grounded in a concrete past, the historical novel lends an aesthetic form to historical experience, employing literary categories like romance and satire, tragedy and comedy, and literary properties, plot, character, setting, thought and diction.[21] The aim is not to tell a true story in the sense of the historian's truth, but a truer one, a poetic or symbolic one. Like history, the historical novel is set in the past. Like biography it is about individuals. But its concern is universalizing. 'The heroes of historical fiction represent not only Renaissance man or Edwardian man but man in general, conceived as a historical being who is subject to the forces of one historical age or another', as Fleishman puts it. 'The ultimate subject of the historical novel is ... man in history, or human life conceived as historical life.'[22]

X. Trapnel, the novelist in Anthony Powell's own *roman fleuve*, declares: 'People think because a novel's invented, it isn't true. Exactly the reverse is the case. Because a novel's

---

[20] Quoted in A. Fleishman, *The English Historical Novel* (Baltimore: Johns Hopkins University Press, 1971), pp.x-xi.
[21] Ibid, p.8.
[22] Ibid., p.11.

invented it is true. Biography and memoirs can never be wholly true, since they can't include every conceivable circumstance of what happened. The novel can do that. The novelist himself lays it down. His decision is binding. The biographer, even at his highest and best, can only be tentative, empirical.'[23] But this does not seem to be true either. For the novelist does not 'lay down every conceivable circumstance', but only what he or she thinks the reader needs to know. 'You may multiply the little facts that can be got from pictures and documents, relics and prints as much as you like, the *real* thing is almost impossible to do', Henry James told Sarah Orne Jewett.[24] The strangeness of past consciousness could not be recovered so easily as its context, if at all.

Historical novels have indeed acquired a new purchase on writers and readers in recent decades. A.S. Byatt, critic as well as novelist, has connected that with 'a complex self-consciousness about the writing of history itself'.[25] Narrative, along with grand narratives, has come to be distrusted: they are just stories. Perhaps it helps to explain the current fashion for biographies of cities, even of other subjects, such as Napalm, or the Antarctic, or the Red Nile. Byatt refers to Hayden White and his interest in 'the refusal of narrative by contemporary historians, who are sensitive to the selective, ideological shapes produced by the narrator, the narrator's designs and beliefs'. The fact, she says, 'that we have in some sense been forbidden to think about history is one reason why so many novelists have taken to it.'[26]

Some of the finest novelists currently writing in English have resorted to this genre, Byatt herself, Pat Barker, Hilary Mantel, Rose Tremain, Timothy Mo, Tash Aw, and, so far as Tasmania's past is concerned, Witi Ihimaera. Historians may well enjoy reading them, but may feel uncomfortable, too. The novelist can do things the historian cannot: he or she can

---

[23] Anthony Powell, *Hearing Secret Harmonies* (London: Heinemann, 1975), p.84.

[24] Quoted in Lowenthal, *The Past is a Foreign Country* , p.230n.

[25] A.S. Byatt, *On Histories and Stories* (London: Vintage, 2001), p.9.

[26] Ibid., pp.10, 11.

tell us what is in their subject's head, what is their motivation, how their heart is beating. And novelists are authorised to shape their narratives. J.G Farrell did his research for *The Singapore Grip*[27] toiling at the British Museum, the Liddell Hart Centre, the Public Record Office, then trying to find remnants of the old Singapore in the new, and going to Saigon to gain a sense of a city under threat.[28] But he could also invent characters to place among those who really existed. Historical novelists can go as far as historians but further, too. Judge not lest ye be judged.

---

[27] *The Singapore Grip* (London: Weidenfeld, 1978).
[28] Lavinia Greacen, *The Making of a Writer* (London: Bloomsbury, 1999), pp.331, 335, 338.

7. On Opera

The historian may have an uncomfortable time at the opera. He or she may be witnessing an Opera based on history that yet distorts it. Mary Stuart did not meet Elizabeth 1, though the duet in Donizetti's opera in which she calls the Queen vile bastard suggests that history missed an opportunity. And Boris Godunov's guilt is less certain than Karamzin, Pushkin, and Mussorgsky suggest.

More often, and perhaps more seriously, the historian may be disturbed by the way in which an opera created in the past is now present to us. In recent decades, presentation has pursued authenticity in respect of the performance of the music, by contrast to earlier practices, according to which, for instance, the words of Weber were altered for the English taste by Henry Bishop in the early 19th century, or, even a century later, Strauss found it necessary to edit *Cosi fan tutti* and *Idomeneo* for German audiences. Authenticity, like objectivity, the historian might add, can never be attained: even if we try to adopt instrumental and vocal practices of the past, they can never sound the same as they did. Most of our opera houses are large, for example, the singers have to be louder and more mature than before. And we have heard a great deal of music since the 18th century. The authenticity movement has, however, justified itself, in particular, perhaps, in giving us so much better an idea of Handel's operas than we had before. Authenticity like objectivity, is an adjective, worth seeking, even if unobtainable. Our ears can take it on.

At the same time, however, staging has generally moved in the opposite direction, particularly in Germany, increasingly elsewhere, and there is little sign that the trend is diminishing. True, attempts to recreate authenticity in this sphere, though they have been made, have been less rewarding than in the musical sphere. Perhaps we have been less ready to adjust our eyes and our ears, and, not surprisingly, we are certainly unready to abandon the electric light the candles gas. True, too, that repetition of the same approaches could become dull and formulaic, particularly as the repertoire of popular operas has become exceedingly limited and offering something fresh requires imagination and inventiveness. But those constraints do not justify the imposition of some 'concept' of the producer or the 'creative team'. Librettist and composer are the true creators.

Sometimes the producer will indeed be offering a criticism of the work given as he or she is seeking to present it to us, and the 'creative team' may become a destructive team, not merely a deconstructive one. That seems to affect the superiority to the past that had little or no justification. At other times, the aim is to offer 'relevance'. But relevance is better sought in more subtle ways than producers are often seen ready to think that audiences are capable of appreciating. Trying to understand what those in the past were attempting to do is more likely to widen our contemporary sympathies and broaden our range of human understanding. In the end the opera-goer may be tempted to conclude that the underlying aim of the producers' opera is to 'shock' and gain notoriety system where, given the narrowness of the repertoire, it can be presumed that, while some like old favourites taken down, others will hate it. Extending the repertoire might be a more artistically profitable exercise, and ultimately perhaps a financially more profitable one. Audiences may tire of a limited repertoire, especially if it has been denatured. Alternatively, or in addition it may be that the 'creative teams' try not to hard, but not hard enough. Sometimes their choices seem to suggest that they have taken the easy way out of the essential dilemma: finding a way of presenting a work that is at once novel but in accordance with its spirit. Sometimes you find that the 'concept' works for a while, and then simply ceases to fit.

If there is a role for the historian at the opera, it is to point out to the historical inaccuracies they may have willingly or unwillingly committed, though the reason they committed them may be interesting and important. But it is a proper task to call for an understanding of what they created. In recreating them and in witnessing the recreations, we may then move beyond the constraints of contemporary relevance, and discover a larger feeling of common humanity, alongside the changes brought by time and social and political circumstance.

The past is a foreign country, L. P. Hartley reminded us. Trying to see it for what it was may help us to understand the foreign far more effectively than insistence upon a localised and short-term relevance.

Too often, it seems, critics have dismissed the libretti of operas as inadequate, if not puerile, while audiences, despairing of understanding what is going on, decide purchase going, as they put it, to listen to the music. These essays are based on the notion that opera is better enjoyed and more satisfying taken seriously, if the stories seem at first sight, and sometimes remain after all, incomprehensible or frivolous. It is hard to find librettists who did not take their work seriously, still harder, perhaps, to find composers. Maybe it is a historian's role to suggest that we may owe them something: at least a degree of respect. Perhaps our debt is a wider one: like other artworks, operas were created in what we would now consider unjust societies. Would we have the operas of Hyden without the vast wealth of the Esterhazy family and the toil of their present neighbours? Would we have *The Ring* without the taxes that enabled the King of Bavaria to indulge in his whims? It was a pity that the politicians did not devise a way of keeping the Kaiser out of politics, too.

Producers and critics, and perhaps historians too, should help members of the audience find their connections with the opera in hand not telling them what its 'relevance' is and not by trying to straitjacket the work, but by enabling them to make their own judgements. An opera after all may have more than one message, if not indeed as many as there are people in the audience. The call is not escapist. It is one for empathy.

However deeply that is achieved, and audiences experience will never be the same as that of the audience at the premiere. That can never be duplicated. But most operas had more than one premiere, and a number entered the repertory, so that a character was inflected by the singers that took them up on the way they stamp roles with something of their own individuality. Performing traditions were built and sometimes broken off. Both processes seem valid enough. Surely indeed it is mainly in this way we might seek an answer to the dilemma. Our productions will be different without wilful attempts to make them so.

Accounts and experiences of this wilfulness - a lavatorial opening to *Un ballo in Maschera*, a rat-infested *Lohengrin*, a pile of dung in *Don Giovanni,* the gathering Valkyries at the Wunderbar, making Calaf Puccini and Zurga colonial governor in love with Nadir - present a temptation to turn with relief to concert performances. Yet concert opera, it might be thought, should fall into the "tinned strawberries" category. Nice enough; have their own flavour; but not the real thing; necessarily only out of season. But if it may be better than nothing, it may also be better than something.

In avoiding production, concert opera avoids producer's concepts. We see chairs on the platform rather than hanging on the wall, and the singers have chairs to sit on rather than having sit on the floor, something rarely done in real life. If we can find no producers with ideas relevant to the opera in hand, we may be better to avoid production. To produce *Les Troyens* with dancers doubling the singers- as if they were not conveying the meaning - his best distraction and at worst an insult. To confine the chorus to head movements and eliminate only the principals' hands suggests a failure of imagination one would rather not witness. Concert performance can allow a concentrated focus on the music, both by performance and audience. Singing Wotan's Farewell with the New Zealand Symphony Orchestra in evening dress on the unadorned platform of the Auckland town Hall, Donald McIntyre made his Brunnhilde weep, and us, too – historians included.

Rather perversely, at a time when the range of operas in the repertoire is so limited, there is a fashion for staging all "semi-staging" works that are not opera: not only *The Damnation of Faust*, which has been subjected to the treatment since Raoul Gunsbourg's days at Monte Carlo, but also the Verdi Requiem and the St Matthew's Passion. It is a work of supererogation. Composers did not expect it or want it. It was also a mistake. While many handle operas are neglected, attempts are made to gauge oratorios, like *Saul* and *Jephtha*. Handel wrote more elaborate choruses when he did not expect to work to be staged. Works in the church style, as

Charles Burney put it, "should partake of choral complication; and the performers having the music before them, are not obliged to get it by heart; whereas an opera chorus, being in action, and committed to memory, must necessarily be short, easy and dramatic".[1] Trying to combine the two may mean that musical accuracy and the coordination are unsustainable, even for the expert choruses that opera houses often now have.

There are positive virtues in concert opera, and they are not all negative. But there is no real substitute for the fully staged work, provided it is done with sympathy. That does not necessarily mean simply "traditional" or naturalistic, nor does it require a non-thinking adherence to the practices of the premiers, recorded in the Paris Opera's *livrets* or in the *disposizione's sceniche* published for the Verdi operas or the minute directions by prepared for the Flying Dutchman. "(T)he canon", as David J. Levin puts it, "retains its vitality through attentive and imaginative readings: it is not served particularly well but either wrote repetition or, for that matter, knee-jerk updating."[2] the production values have to take real account of the work in hand and the purpose of its creators. And to ensure that may be the work, not only are producers of performance, critics, audiences, and historians.

---

[1] Quoted in Ian Woodfield, *Opera and Drama in Eighteenth-century London* (Cambridge: Cambridge University Press, 2001), p.43.

[2] David J. Levin, *Unsettling Opera Staging Mozart, Verdi, Wagner, and Zemlinsky* (Chicago: University of Chicago Press, 2007), p.66

8. On Time and Place

'Time has no divisions to mark its passage, there is never a thunderstorm or blare of trumpets to announce the beginning of a new month or year. Even when a new century begins it is only we mortals who ring bells and fire off pistols.'[1] We mortals differ in the way we divide up time. Those differences themselves altered over time.

In the oral environments Barbara Andaya describes in her work on South-east Sumatra, stories were handed down from the past: they were 'ever-mutating', but 'perceived as unchanging'.[2] There was no sense of sequential time. Lucien Pye felt that "the Burmese lack any feeling for tidiness in history; they do not see history in terms of stages or phases, and so they are not led to see one sequence rounded off before the next is begun".[3] 'What could provide a time-referent for different groups', Barbara Andaya continued, '... was the reign of a common overlord'.[4] The lives of Kings could present 'a means of identifying a shared block of time'.[5] That, of course, remained a common concept in other societies, in Europe and elsewhere, where there was a greater sense of the passage of time. One lived in Good King Charles' Golden Days or in the Meiji era.

Such a view of the passage of time sometimes had, both in Asian and European societies, another dimension: the concept of decline and restoration. It suggested that change was neither evolutionary nor, except in a special sense, revolutionary. The Meiji Restoration encapsulates the notion. But such a view was not peculiar to Asia. It had not been uncommon in Renaissance Europe: indeed the concept of

---

[1] Thomas Mann, *The Magic Mountain*, London: Minerva, ch.5.
[2] B. Andaya, *To Live as Brothers* (Honolulu: Hawaii University Press, 1993), p.8.
[3] Lucien W. Pye, *Politics, Personality and Nation Building*, New Haven: Yale University Press 1962, p.167.
[4] Andaya, *To Live as Brothers*, p.11.
[5] Ibid., p.112.

renaissance is not incompatible with it. Machiavelli's *Discorsi* may itself have been recapturing the attitude of the Romans, and his own *Il Principe* did not follow the same pattern. But something of the same approach was evident in the English revolution. It aimed to restore the time passed.

> every age
> Appears to souls who live every age in't (ask Carlyle)
> Most heroic. Ours, for instance, ours…
> A pewter age - mixed metal, silver washed;
> Age of scum, spooned off the richer past.
> (E. B. Browning, *Aurora Leigh*)

Nonetheless more linear view of time had begun to prevail. Time could now be saved and wasted. The idea of progress, the subject of an eponymously titled book by J. B. Berry,[6] overlaid and reinforced it. The French revolutionaries decided that a new era had started, Year 1. Even those countries that counted by regnal years accepted that their history was a lineal one, moving from Rama III to Rama IV, or indeed from Meiji to Taisho. Sir John Plumb proclaimed in 1963 that 'if there is one idea that makes sense of history, it is the idea of progress . . . The world is less savage, less brutal, less tyrannical than it was one hundred years ago.'[7]

Reigns have yet remained useful to historians, as labels, as characterising descriptions, such as the Victorian Era. An alternative is to use Christian centuries. Perhaps it was only in the last one that the end of the century was associated with decadence, *'fin de siècle'*, 'a kind of decimal determinism'.[8] Sometimes centuries are stretched to suit, for example, Braudel's long sixteenth or Hobsbawm's short twentieth.

If most mortals like to break up time, writers have to. How are 'abridgements' otherwise to be made a manageable?

---

[6] J.B. Bury, *The Idea of Progress* (New York: Macmillan, 1932 [1921]).

[7] J.H. Plumb, *Sunday Times Weekly Review*, 10 March 1963.

[8] D. Lowenthal, *The Past is a Foreign Country*, Cambridge: Cambridge University Press, 1985, p. 221.

Butterfield asked. 'The difficulty of the general historian is that he has to abridge and that he must do it without altering the meaning and the peculiar message of history . . . '[9] Things have to be left out: but abridgement must not do violence to the complexity of the historical process. Too often, textbook writers were at fault, compiling indeed from other abridgements. Abridgement had to maintain 'texture' of history.[10]

More recently, French historians have attempted an alternative approach, splitting time, as it were, horizontally rather than vertically. For Braudel, time, like Gaul or the Almighty, could be divided into three parts . . . The short term produced the 'event', the middling the 'conjuncture', and from the long duration came the 'structure'.[11]

Both approaches, vertical and horizontal, have their dangers. What may seem the inconvenience of the first can be an inconvenience. If the historian is seeking explanations, they will not be readily confined within a chronological framework. Even in a single state, changes are sure to be too complex to be aptly related to the activities of even the strongest monarch. If the century has to be compressed or stretched, what validity has it as descriptor or a divider?

The second approach risks in balance in the relationship of the long-term and the contingent. It may underplay the events - often political - in favour of the continuities, and diminish the political, even though the political may be part of the context. It is a guide to thinking about the problems of writing history. But it can be as inadequate as a 'narrative' can be.

Both approaches, of course, are tied to prescriptions about what is significant or important that has occurred over time. '. . . periods are modes of dealing with specific questions and must change with the questions', Anthony Reid has

---

[9] H. Butterfield, *The Whig Interpretation of History* (London: Bell, 1931), p.22.

[10] Ibid., p.103

[11] R.J.B. Bosworth, *Explaining Auschwitz and Hiroshima* (London: Routledge, 1993), p.105.

declared.[12] Adopting a time-frame may be the result of a decision as to what is important, or it may lead to a decision as to what is important. Writing a general text is likely to fall, into the first category. The problem is to do that without falling, or appearing to fall, into the second.

The only valid approach is perhaps what might be called the 'health warning' approach. Bear in mind the nature of the historiographical enterprise. No book offers the final word. No structure will comprise the whole mansion. No explanation will be complete. No time-lines will do justice to a story that has a beginning but no beginning and an end but no end.

If these counsels create difficulty for a singly authored work, they are even more so when applied to a multi-authored one. Such may have to be divided volume from volume, as well as contribution from contribution. Contribution may be divided from contribution by content as well as time-frame. There will be no answer appropriate to all the topics, let alone one that satisfies all the authors or all their readers. The editor will be criticised; haunted, too, by the fear that decisions that had to be arbitrary have become the guiding principles, if not of the authors, then of the students and the teachers who use the work in first coming to terms with the history or histories concerned.

In the 1950s and the 1960s, when independent states had just been set up or were being set up, there was a concern, too, to de-colonise historiography. John Bastin and his critics discussed the 'Western element' in South-east Asian in historiography, and John Smail conceived of 'autonomous' histories. At times the contending parties went too far. 'Taken to the extreme, autonomous histories that push the colonizers or their elite collaborators into the shadows would produce the same distortions as do colonial histories that push the

---

[12] A. Reid, *Southeast Asia in the Age of Commerce*, New Haven: Yale University Press, 1993, II, p.xiv.

"natives" or subaltern groups into the shadow', as Laurie Sears has recognised.[13]

The historians of several Southeast Asian states are now concerned to write 'national' history. What might be is a subject of much discussion in the profession. Is it a history designed to serve a 'national' purpose? That seems to be one facet of it, and the search for a book or books that might be used in schools and in junior university courses seems to point the way. For some, however, it goes further than that. It is an assertion that history cannot be written by other than 'nationals' can only be written in the 'national' language. That case has been put strongly by some of the historians at the University of the Philippines and by others in Thailand and in Brunei Darussalam. It represents in some sense a recrudescence of views that were common in the decolonisation period of the 1950s and 1960s. Now 'decolonisation' is not an issue, but 'globalisation' may be. Nations not only seek to boost their unity, but also their distinctiveness. The 'global village' is not in prospect. Or if it is, each house will have assertively different architecture and its own garden to cultivate.

Edward Said has expressed his concern. 'If one believes with Gramsci that an intellectual vocation is socially possible as well as desirable, then it is an inadmissible contradiction the same time to build analyses of historical experience around exclusions that stipulate, for instance, that only women can understand feminine experience, only Jews can understand Jewish suffering, only formally colonial subjects can understand colonial experience.'[14]

An historian may well wonder where this places the profession that is emerged, in Europe, in the US, in Australasia, in Southeast Asia itself, in the twentieth century. Writing textbooks is bound, as Butterfield put it, to

---

[13] Laurie J. Sears, *Autonomous Histories, Particular Truths, Madison*: Centre for Southeast Asian Studies, University of Wisconsin, 1993, pp.17-18.

[14] Edward Said *Culture and Imperialism*, New York: Knopf, 1993, p.31.

'foreshortened' history: indeed, he argues that the mechanics of the task ensured the adoption of what he called a Whig interpretation. 'Presentism' is certainly a danger. How is the historian going to structure, to periodise, to resource, the history of a country the frontiers of which may be only recent, the heroes of which may have fought each other, the cultures of which are diverse? It is, after all, striking how few satisfactory histories there are of that strange agglomeration, the UK. It could not have a 'unified historiography', J. G. A. Pocock has argued.[15] Is there not a tendency to write the history of Britain as if it were the history of England? How indeed is the history of Scotland and of Wales to be part of the 'national' history?

'Too close a concern with the remembered past of various Indonesian peoples always threatened to endanger rather than confirm the newly defined unity', Tony Reid has observed in respect of the history-writing of the early revolution.[16] The structural problems for the historian must also lead to a questioning of the political purpose. If that is to create a sense of nationhood, it is necessary to ask if it is to be a history of the predominant element in the modern state. Might not a sense of belonging be best ensured by national history once more subtle and more inclusive?

Nor is the notion that 'national' history is 'nationalised' history a happy thought. It is true that overwhelmingly the history of England has been written by the English and that of the US by Americans. But the insights of others have often been profoundly helpful. Could English history of the eighteenth century ever be the same after Lewis Namier? Does not Paul Kennedy tell us something of the US?

There is a political issue here, too. Nations will have to live with nations, rather than furiously rage together. Assertive national histories will prejudice such a prospect. A sense of

---

[15] *American Historical Review*, 87 (1982), p.331.

[16] A. Reid in A. Read and David Marr eds, *Perception of the Past in Southeast Asia* (Singapore: Heinemann, 1979), pp. 297-8.

nationhood is after all born of knowing others as well as oneself.

The writing of the history of Southeast Asia, and of countries within Southeast Asia, has advanced immeasurably, if irregularly, since the war. It has been stimulated not only by political change and by the expansion of education. Its own controversies have been stimulating. New evidence has been made available. New approaches have been adopted. It has been a world-wide endeavour, not merely a national one. Surely it has been the better for that. The approach of Braudel to the Mediterranean past inspired the New Zealander/Australian Tony Reid to tackle the Age of Commerce in Southeast Asia. He was no doubt inspired, too, by the relevance of that age of commerce to the present one.

Like the present author, Prof Reid adopted a regional approach. That is also controversial. What relationship do the individual states have to their neighbours? In what sense, if any, do their people see themselves as Southeast Asian? The historiographical issues that the concept raises are again both a reflection of the contemporary issues and a contribution to the discussion of them.

This chapter was taken from the book Nicholas Tarling, Nations and States in South-east Asia *(Auckland: New Zealand Asia Institute, University of Auckland, 1998).*

9. On Popular Culture (in History and Theory)

Historians are famous or notorious for their alleged distaste or distrust of theory, though sometimes claiming, as did my late colleague, Sir Keith Sinclair, that it is there all the same, but concealed.[1] Perhaps it is strange, but this historian, albeit of an older generation, feels he needs some theory, or at least some definition, especially when a genre with which one is unfamiliar, as is the case here: my topic being popular culture as it figures in international relations in Asia now and in the future. It is a topic on which one might expect the historian to have something to say, but first it seems necessary to address the question of the theoretical frame within which one might begin.

It is indeed a large task. But turning over such literature as I could, I found that experienced colleagues in that field often seem to do without definition. Their cover many topics - from rock and rap musicians to TV ads and gangster movies - without necessarily suggesting what is common to them or what distinguishes them from other forms of culture. Its omnipresence seems, as Ian Craven says,[2] to be an obstacle to interpretation: the critic drowns in data.

Perhaps indeed the definition might be a negative one. It is everything that is not non-popular. It is, in Peter Burke's phrase, 'unofficial culture, the culture of the non-elite'.[3] But then I want a definition of everything it is not. Is its opposite 'elite' culture or is it 'high' or 'dominant' culture? Is 'popular culture' different from 'mass' culture? Has it any features that

---

[1] Sinclair, Keith, *Halfway Round the Harbour: An Autobiography*, (Auckland: Penguin,1993), p.177.

[2] Ian Craven *et al.* (eds.), *Australian Popular Culture* (Cambridge: Cambridge University Press, 1994), p.4.

[3] Quoted by Günther Lottes in Steven L. Kaplan (ed.), *Understanding Popular Culture* (Berlin: Mouton, 1984), p.147.

were exclusive to it? Is it indeed completely exclusive? Or has it features in common with 'elite', 'high', or 'mass culture'? Maybe no agreement is to be expected. For Steven Kaplan in 1984, the notion of popular culture was 'clouded by conceptual uncertainties'.[4] 'The historian of popular culture is in pursuit of an elusive quarry', wrote David Hill.[5]

In our task, focused on the actuality and prospect of a regionalisation of popular culture, we must include assessing the impact in Asia, actual and potential, of a popular culture deeply inflected by the experience and invention of the West. Of that process, however, there seems to be still less theory, though some research. It leads to the conclusion that, in the absence of a definition, it might be helpful briefly to traverse the story and study of popular culture in the West. That might give us a basis for tackling our task in the East.

The story and study are, of course, not undertaken within popular culture. It is rather the object of study by the tellers of story among the elite rather than the mass. We must expect it to be affected by their concerns, even their prejudices for and against it, even if they are interviewing its exponents. '[T]he very 'lowest' of popular culture has increasingly attracted attention from the very 'highest' of theoretical positions.'[6] That has often been accompanied by a recondite jargon.

What first came to mind are the works of historians of the inter-war and post-war periods - those associated with *Annales*, with *Past and Present*, R. H. Tawney, Eileen Power, the Hammonds—who tried to turn us away from the history of kings and queens - and great power diplomacy – from 1066 and all that - and encouraged us by precept and example to consider those the rulers tried to rule. Quite often their history was inspired by their sympathy with the village labourer, the working classes, the trade union movement, if not by Marxist ideology. What inspired them? The rise of Labour? Their knowledge of Marxism?

---

[4] Ibid., Preface, p. 1.

[5] Ibid., p.57.

[6] Ian Craven *et al* (eds), *Australian Popular Culture*, p.10.

And maybe some approaches are still associated with 'class' analyses unduly closely. A case in point is the work of the Birmingham Cultural Studies Centre. It has been seen to adopt 'a somewhat rigidly Marxist framework which privileges class over all other constituents of cultural identity'. A distinction is drawn between sub-cultures and the 'mainstream': 'The former are defined by their active and authentic resistance and the latter as passive and manipulated.'[7] Such an approach seems to Matsue and others 'too limiting in its heavy emphasis on hegemonic relations between the dominant and subordinate groups, not allowing for momentary participation, nor fully appreciating the existence of shared values between groups. … In essence, the subcultural approach often is too fixed, and it is often too loaded within academics [(sic)] in its association with issues of class'.[8] To others, such as Rehan Hyder, it seems to neglect the sense of individuality, even though that forms part of sub-cultural identity.[9]

The movement dealt with earlier periods, too, however. Colleagues were, for example, fascinated by the witchcraft of the seventeenth century CE and its opponents. Some were able to re-create the individual lives of peasants and the milieu of town-workers. 'A journeyman's initiation rite, a village festive organization, an informal gathering of women for a lying-in or of men and women for story-telling, or a street disturbance could be 'read' as fruitfully as a diary, a political tract, a sermon, or a body of laws.'[10] Colleagues were fascinated, too, by 'carnival', activities that inverted the ordinary rules of social control, willingly, however, accepted

---

[7] Rehan Hyder, *Brimful of Asia* (Aldershot: Ashgate, 2004), p.35.

[8] Jennifer Miloto Matsue, *Making Music in Japan's Underground* (New York: Routledge, 2009), p.33.

[9] Rehan Hyder, *Brimful of Asia*, p.36.

[10] Natalie Davis, *Society and Culture in Early Modern France*, (Stanford: Stanford University Press, 1975), pp.xv1-xv11.

by elites 'in order to release tensions that could otherwise be threatening'.[11]

Those projects still do not, however, take us far enough back in the history of historians interested in something that might be called popular culture and so perhaps helping to define it by exclusion or inclusion. Should I consider those who concerned themselves with 'folk' culture? Or is that something else again? It might well be regarded as 'popular' culture, but a form that was, or was taken to be, more deep-rooted, less changeable, if not unchanging.

That topic had interested a learned elite in Europe, I suppose, ever since a secular elite emerged and began to publish books. But this line of thinking also brings me forward in time, to those with a more urgent motive than the scholarly. German scholars in particular sought to invoke the *Volk*, if not invent it, in part as a reaction against the incursions of the French revolution and Napoleon, rather as the French were to look to the *longue durée* in the Vichy period.

The brothers Jacob and Wilhelm Grimm produced collections that became world-famous, but their initial aim was different, and the 'fairy' tales were not for children. Of modest social standing, they identified with the common hard-working people. They were also driven by political events, above all the French invasions of the disunited Germany of the early nineteenth century.

'[T]he ardour with which we pursued the studies of Old German helped us to overcome the spiritual depression of those days. Without doubt, world events and the need to retire into the space of research, contributed to the re-discovery of this long-forgotten literature.'[12] Their aim was to recover the 'natural essence' of the Germans from the medieval past, and so build a more authentic united Germany. '[T]heir desire to publish a work which expressed a German cultural spirit was

---

[11] David Hall, 'Introduction', in Steven L. Kaplan (ed.), *Understanding Popular Culture*, p.11.

[12] Quoted in Jack Zipes, *The Brothers Grimm* (Basingstoke: Palgrave, 2002), p.7.

part of an effort to contribute to a united German front against the French.'[13]

Their study was pursued in the 'romantic' atmosphere associated with Johann Gottfried Herder, for whom folk songs and poems had been the 'archives of a nationality', 'imprints of the national soul', the 'living voice of nationalities, nay, even of humanity itself'.[14] '[F]olk poesie', Wilhelm Grimm maintained, 'stems from the soul of the entire community.' The new poetry names its poets, 'the old knows none to name'.[15] In fact, it is now realised, the Grimms listened to storytellers who came to their house, often quite educated people, and many of the tales they told were influenced, paradoxically enough, by the French tradition and by their wide reading. In turn they were to re-shape the tales so that ultimately they became something you could read to middle-class children.

The *Völkisch* also became, on the other hand, the inspiration for a nationalism that was to turn violent and aggressive. But, though there were similar attempts to see the people as uniquely the preservers of a national past, they did not all follow that route. In France itself - perhaps another paradox - '[t]he seductive conflation of national identity and popular culture' was established from the late 1820s.[16] But the Russian populists, *narodniki*, looked to 'the people' for inspiration against what was seen as an oppressive and alien Tsardom. They were indeed to develop a terrorist wing that was responsible for the assassination of Alexander II. But there was a more sentimental side to it, echoed by the establishment composer Tchaikovsky when he tried to give his fourth symphony a programme. 'The fourth movement [which quotes a folk-song]. If within yourself you find no reasons for joy, look at others. Go among the people. ... O,

---

[13] Ibid., p.111.

[14] Paul A. Reynolds, *Prometheus in Music* (Aldershot: Ashgate, 2007), p.145.

[15] Quoted in Jack Zipes, *The Brothers Grimm*, p.11.

[16] Annegret Fauser, *Musical Encounters at the 1889 Paris World's Fair* (Rochester: Rochester University Press, 2005), p.254.

how they are enjoying themselves, how happy they are that all their feelings are simple and direct!'[17]

Alexander II's statue stands in Helsinki, the only statue to a Tsar. Under Russian rule the Finnish language was encouraged to emerge from Swedish dominance, and in 1835 Elias Lönnrot published the *Kalevala*, the epic that was to inspire Sibelius. But again it was so much a collation that it was more or less an invention. In Hungary Ferenc Erkel deployed *verbunkos* as if it were genuine folk music, though much of it derived from the recruiting music of the eighteenth-century Habsburg army. Fifty years later Bartók and Kodaly sought the genuine article and made it a basis for their music.

Something similar occurred in England, where the Folk Song Society was founded in 1898. There was no great political issue involved in evoking or reinventing the popular past in music or story. But the advance of industrial society and the destruction of a partly imagined rural life induced Cecil Sharp, Gustav Holst, and Ralph Vaughan Williams to collect English folk-song before it died out in the face of a different kind of popular culture. '[W]hatever is done in the way of preserving traditional music must be done quickly', Vaughan Williams declared in 1904; 'it must be remembered that the tunes, at all events, of true folk tunes exist only by oral tradition, so that if they are not soon noted down and preserved they will be lost forever'. He remarked on 'the evident antiquity of many of the tunes' that he had noted down, 'many of them being founded on the old 'Church modes''.[18]

For Vaughan Williams, as for Bartók, folk music was an inspiration and a fruitful legacy. Others felt only a sense of loss. F.R. Leavis insisted that there was in the seventeenth century 'a real culture of the people ... a positive culture

---

[17] Quoted in David Brown, *The Crisis Years* (London: Gollancz, 1982), p.166.

[18] Quoted in Ursula Vaughan Williams, *R.V.W.: A Biography of Ralph Vaughan Williams* (Oxford: Oxford University Press, 1988), p.70.

which has disappeared'. 'What we have lost is the organic community with the living culture it embodied.'[19] He is echoed, perhaps surprisingly, by the American neo-Marxist Fredric Jameson, who referred to 'the older kinds of folk and genuinely 'popular' culture which flourished when the older social classes of a peasantry and an urban *artisanat* still existed and which, from the nineteenth century on, have gradually been colonised and extinguished by commodification and the market system'.[20]

Some of what had taken place was clearly a matter of 'appropriation'. The elite was finding what it wanted to find among 'the people', even inventing what it hoped or expected to find. Another example is the waltz, which rose from humble origins to the heights of society, like Cinderella [Aschenbrodel]. But the borrowing was not all one-way. Popular notions were sometimes versions of elite concepts. 'What qualifies as folklore may have originated in systems, sometimes learned, sometimes not, that long since disintegrated.'[21] Erkel certainly heard *verbunkos* in the villages, and Vaughan Williams detected the church modes in some of the songs he collected. Some Venetian gondoliers allegedly memorised the whole of Tasso's epic poem *Gerusalemme Liberata*.[22] '[E]ach cultural form is a mixture, whose constituent elements meld together indissolubly.'[23] 'Cultural consumption, whether popular or not, is at the same time a form of production, which creates ways of using that cannot

---

[19] Quoted in John Storey, *Cultural Theory and Popular Culture* (Athens: University of Georgia Press, 2006), pp.20, 50.

[20] Quoted in ibid., p.137

[21] David Hall, "Introduction", in Steven L. Kaplan (ed.), *Understanding Popular Culture*, p. 9.

[22] John Rosselli, *Music and Musicians in Nineteenth-century Italy* (London: Batsford, 1991), p.25.

[23] Roger Chartier, quoted in David Hall, "Introduction", in Steven L. Kaplan (ed.), *Understanding Popular Culture*, p. 13.

be limited to the intentions of those who produce.'[24] Which process of appropriation or borrowing - if either - applies in the post-modern world Jameson criticises?

My explorations as an historian differ, it seems, from those of cultural theorists. The industrial revolution abuts only on part of my discourse. But for them the industrial revolution is central. The 'organising principle' of Raymond Williams' *Culture and Society*, as the author tells us, 'is the discovery that the idea of culture, and the word itself in its general modern uses, came into English thinking in the period which we commonly describe as that of the Industrial Revolution'.[25] There are other ways to define culture, John Storey admits when he quotes this, but they are 'definitions which fall outside the range of the cultural theorists and the cultural theory' he discusses in his book, which is defined by 'there being in place a market economy'. By admitting that change, he admits, of course, that there were earlier forms of 'popular culture', though the words may not have been used. To an historian it seems important not to cut out the consideration of earlier forms to which the words might well apply, and which certainly forms at the least a useful comparator. Indeed Storey himself quotes the preface to E.P. Thompson's *The Making of the English Working Class* where the author describes his intention of rescuing those who opposed the revolution— the Luddites, the handloom weavers, the 'utopian' artisans, the followers of Joanna Southcott - from 'the enormous condescension of posterity'. He also discusses the Caribbean,[26] hardly a site for industrial revolution. And Kaplan's book covers the 'early modern' period.

Undoubtedly the industrial revolution, starting in Britain, produced vast social change, a sense of there being two 'nations' rather than one, as Egremont's interlocutor puts it in

---

[24] Roger Chartier, "Culture as Appropriation: Popular Cultural Uses in Early Modern France", in Steven L. Kaplan (ed.), *Understanding Popular Culture*, p. 234.

[25] Quoted in John Storey, *Cultural Theory and Popular Culture*, p.10

[26] John Storey, ibid, pp.39, 64.

Disraeli's novel *Sybil*, 'the rich and the poor', 'between whom there is no intercourse and no sympathy, … who are formed by a different breeding, are fed by a different food, are ordered by different manners, and are not governed by the same laws'.[27] Not surprisingly it produced apprehension, a fear of 'anarchy'. But pre-industrial elites, if less fearful, had hypothesised a popular culture, and found a use for it. Of the theorists, Antonio Gramsci seems the most persuasive to an historian, though he employs words in new senses. The concept of 'hegemony' is, perhaps, in itself too rigid. What appeals more is what he calls - not very aptly in the eyes of a diplomatic historian - 'negotiations' between dominant and subordinate groups, a process marked by 'resistance' and 'incorporation'. Culture is not imposed from above, nor does it emerge spontaneously from below. It is a mix, a shifting balance, 'a compromise equilibrium', as Gramsci put it.[28]

Fortified by these investigations, which provide some sort of taxonomy if not with explicit definitions, I can turn back to Asia, where few seem to have tried to deploy the theories developed in respect of Western societies, let alone considered the question of regionalisation. There is of course an added complication: the colonial/globalising relationships and the reaction to them; and now the increased mobility of popular culture, involving 'the circulation of texts, fashions, styles and even 'attitudes', across widely different cultural spaces'.[29]

Here again you—or the historian in you—have to consider what happened, and what was and is said to have happened. And you may also need to consider whether those saying it are from the West or educated in Western disciplines.

Even a short survey seems to offer many close comparisons, provided we are not compelled to wait for the industrial revolution. It would be hard to ignore the concept of the Great Tradition and the Little Tradition in China, nor

---

[27] B. Disraeli, *Sybil* (Oxford: Oxford University Press, 1981[1845]), pp.65–6.

[28] John Storey, *Cultural Theory and Popular Culture*, p. 65.

[29] Ian Craven *et al.* (eds.), *Australian Popular Culture*, p.1.

the extent to which, though distinct, the latter borrows from the former. Alexander Woodside's Nguyen dynasts in Vietnam fight against the Little Tradition in their Southeast Asian lands with their concept of the Great Tradition. Ray Ileto's peasants witness their version of Christ's redemptive message in the *pasyon* (passion) plays.

In colonial times both the division and the appropriation take new forms. Both mass and elite borrow from the new colonialist elite, willy-nilly. But the nationalist elite also borrows from the masses, rather as the European nationalists had done. They speak for the 'people' - for Sukarno's Marhaen, his typified peasant, for example - and try to assimilate their often Europe-derived concepts to 'traditional' aspirations. The result, as the Indonesians found on more than one occasion, could be devastating. In the early 1920s, for example, the Partai Komunis Indonesia, finding it difficult to organise the unions, and facing government repression, turned to the countryside. Its leaders were themselves seized by the popular utopianism they evoked. The *djoboyo* prophecy – which seemed to foretell the departure of the Dutch - was identified with the Soviet Union and the revolution identified with the coming of the *ratu adil* or just prince. Later the left-wing nationalists in Portuguese Timor, Fretilin, began by using the native languages, not Portuguese, and appropriated Mau-bere, a term of contempt in the Mambai language for poor peasants.[30]

In the Philippines, where Western education was introduced earlier than elsewhere in Southeast Asia, an elite formulated a nationalism in the way it was done in Europe. The great polymath José Rizal edited Antonio de Morga's contemporary account of the islands at the time the Spaniards first established their control. But if that might appeal to the intellectuals, his personality acquired a popular charisma. Advised to leave the Philippines, he found his absence only intensified the 'popular textualisation' of his career. 'Alas,

---

[30] Helen Hill, *Fretilin: The Origins, Ideologies and Strategies of a Nationalist Movement in East Timor*, MA thesis, Monash University, 1978, p.86.

José!' a townmate wrote to him in 1889. 'All the people here ask about you and pin their hope on you. Even the poorest people of the mountains are asking about your return. It seems that they consider you the second Jesus who will liberate them from misery!'[31]

Nationalism does not end with independence. It becomes a matter of state-building, and you can witness transitions in popular culture, for example, in the case of *Bangsawan*: the popular Malay theatre brought to the Peninsula by immigrant groups, subsequently urbanised, and then becoming a national form.[32] But the state-building is done in a world very different from the world

of the nineteenth-century European nationalists. The world after the Second World War becomes a world of states, equal in sovereignty, very unequal in power. It is also a world with an unprecedented degree of international exchange and communication in almost every field. The most powerful of the states, the United States, contributes powerfully to a highly commercialised celebrity-oriented mass culture. By what means?

The notion of 'mass culture' is associated in the historian's mind with the debate in the United States of the 1950s, though it is linked, too, to the approach of Leavis and others in the UK. Bernard Rosenberg and David

Manning White edited *Mass Culture: The Popular Arts in America,* published in 1957. 'At worst', wrote Rosenberg, 'mass culture threatens not merely to cretinize our taste, but to brutalize our senses while paving the way to totalitarianism.'[33] Mass culture, Dwight Macdonald argued, was a parasitic culture, feeding on high culture, offering nothing in return. 'Folk art grew from below. It was a

---

[31] Quoted in Reynaldo Ileto, *Pasyon and Revolution* (Quezon City: Ateneo de Manila Press, 1979), p.313.

[32] Jan van der Putten, "Negotiating the Great Depression: The Rise of Popular Culture and Consumerism in Early-1930s Malaya", *Journal of Southeast Asian Studies*, 41 (2010), p.23.

[33] Quoted in John Storey, *Cultural Theory and Popular Culture*, p.22.

spontaneous, autochthonous expression of the people, shaped by themselves, pretty much without the benefit of High Culture, to suit their needs. Mass culture is imposed from above. It is fabricated by technicians hired by businessmen; its audience are passive consumers, their participation limited to the choice of buying and not buying.' Mass culture, he declared, integrated the masses into 'a debased form of high culture', and so became 'an instrument of political domination'.[34]

The concept may also be associated with the views of the Frankfurt School, a group of intellectuals who moved to New York when Hitler came to power, including men like Theodor Adorno, Max Horkheimer, Walter Benjamin, and Herbert Marcuse. Horkheimer and Adorno coined the term 'culture industry'. That, they thought, was marked by 'conformity' and 'predictability': you know how the film will end, what turn the hit song will take. Perhaps their experience of Germany encouraged the School to perceive 'the deceived masses' as caught in a 'circle of manipulation and retroactive need in which the unity of the system grows ever stronger'.[35]

But, before turning back to Asia, consider, in the light of the earlier discussion, two possible criticisms. The first issue is the question of political domination. Perhaps that was apparent to the Frankfurters. What did Macdonald mean? Though he had referred to businessmen, he claimed that the Soviet Union was even more the land of 'mass culture' than the United States. There indeed you might detect 'political domination'. But is it so evident in the capitalist economy? The object of the 'culture industry', like that of other industries, was to make a profit. In whose hands, if any, does hegemony lie?

Second, the hegemony may, after all, be 'negotiated'. Are the masses merely manipulated even by the power of the 'culture industry'? Post-Marxist cultural studies reject the notion that 'the people' are 'cultural dupes', victims of 'an up-dated form of the opium of the people'. Fiske offers a kind of

---

[34] Quoted in ibid., p. 10.
[35] Ibid., p. 49.

'semiotic guerrilla warfare', in which 'the hegemonic forces of homogeneity are always met by the resistances of heterogeneity'. Films are 'read' in ways that their makers do not expect. Michel de Certeau goes so far as to identify 'consumption' as 'secondary production'. Even a fan culture is not merely a matter of mere consumption. '[T]he picture of young people as innocents exploited by the pop industry', Hall and Whannel admit, is 'over-simplified'.[36] '[C]ultural meanings', Roy Shuker suggests, 'are ultimately made by consumers, even if this process is under conditions and opportunities not of their own making'.[37]

With such questions in mind, look East again. May we borrow the vertical Gramsci-type concept for the lateral West–Asia relationship, or more generally for examining the globalisation of popular and mass culture? Is there not another - perhaps overlapping - 'compromise equilibrium'? There are Western borrowings from Asia, some more authentic than others, as there have been in high culture, in pottery, in music, in poetry. The Beatles incorporated Indian music, and karate films inspired rap. And in Asia there are Gramsci-type counter-currents to 'Americanisation', itself, of course, really no monolith. Rap, perhaps unexpectedly, appealed in Tokyo, but it was J-rap. Hybridisation, the formulation of the critical theorists, seems inadequate as a description, let alone as an explanation of process.

It seems that pop culture will largely displace the equivalent of the folk cultures that Vaughan Williams and others sought to preserve in Europe, where, with Peter, Paul and Mary, 'folk' has itself come to be something quite different.[38] What will emerge, however, is not a single global culture, but rather a global culture inflected with the local, global, as some have termed it, borrowing Roland Robertson's coinage. '[W]hat we usually call the global, far from being something which, in a systematic fashion, rolls

---

[36] 36 Ibid., pp. 69, 158, 161, 163, 42.
[37] Roy Shuker, *Understanding Popular Music Culture* (Abingdon, New York: Routledge, 2013), pp.79–80.
[38] Ibid., p.57.

over everything, creating similarity, in fact works through particularity. ... There is always a dialectic, between the local and the global.'[39]

This is a culture not readily turned to account by nation-builders. Stalin tried to ban the saxophone. There is another dialectic. Power-holders may try Tony Blair-style rather desperately to capture some of the popularity of popular culture by association, and/or they may seek to limit any subversive qualities it may have. The most common subaltern response to the elite's cultural managers in Thailand is to opt for what they consider 'excessive' Westernisation.[40] Governments may seek to preserve their folk cultures as a demonstration of concern for minorities and as a means of attracting tourists. There they will find something 'different', though scarcely 'authentic'. But, whatever the political view, the capitalists' priority will be profit.

Art forms have to be distinguished not only by the way they appeal to senses, but also in the manner of conception and propagation. A major painting may exist only in one copy, possibly acquiring immense value - though it rarely accrues to the painter - and the rest of us have to be content with prints or visits to a gallery. A book, if it gets into the market, may become a best-seller or be remaindered. Composers produce music that has to be performed by others, but may be endlessly repeated, live or dead. Films are often expensive and risky to produce and difficult to distribute. Two forms seem to be particularly prominent in discussion of pop culture: viz. music and film/TV. And the nature of their conception and propagation is no doubt relevant.

---

[39] Stuart Hall, quoted in John Storey, *Cultural Theory and Popular Culture*, p.151.

[40] Peter A. Jackson, "Afterword: Postcolonial Theories and Thai Semicolonial Hybridities", in Rachel V. Harrison and Peter A. Jackson (eds.), *The Ambiguous Allure of the West: Traces of the Colonial in Thailand* (Hong Kong: Hong Kong University Press, 2010), p.202.

Film, as Gerben Bakker puts it, industrialised mass entertainment by making it tradable.[41] He and Dominic Strinati have traced some of the steps in its development and its globalisation. One of the key factors was the high sunk cost. That made for the success of the United States, with its large domestic market, as Pathé, the French film-maker, lamented in 1940. 'Having the advantage of their huge interior market, which, concerning box office revenue, represents forty to fifty times the French one, thus three quarters of the world market, the Americans can engage considerable sums in the production of their negatives, amortise them completely in their home market, and subsequently conquer the export markets all over the world, especially those of countries that cannot afford the luxury of having their own national film production.'[42]

The industry came to be dominated by a few major corporations, not so much because of their interest in production, as because of their control of distribution and exhibition. They survived the depression, in part by deploying the B movie and the double-feature,[43] and the Second World War was a boom time. King George V wondered if anything could be done about the 'deplorable effect of cinema pictures on the prestige of the European in the Far East'.[44] It is hard to estimate how much the world-wide distribution of US films contributed to a world-wide wish to share the 'American dream'.

Post-war the industry had to contend with trust-busters and with competition from new forms of entertainment, in particular TV. Its answers partly lay in the different methods of production, including the abandonment of the studio

---

[41] Gerben Bakker, *Entertainment Industrialised: The Emergence of the International Film Industry, 1890–1940* (Cambridge: Cambridge University Press, 2009), p.2.

[42] Quoted in ibid., p.222.

[43] Dominic Strinati, *An Introduction to Studying Popular Culture* (London: Routledge, 2000), p.16

[44] Quoted in John A. Lent, *The Asian Film Industry* (Austin: University of Texas Press, 1990), p.186.

system for the 'package' system. It also lay in finding fashionable genres, including the blockbuster and, most recently, the deployment of special effects, where New Zealand has in recent decades found a niche.

What is the relationship between the development of such genres and developments in society itself? Strinati questions a 'reflectionist' interpretation. That relies, as he says, on a liberal and pluralist view of society that argued 'that its culture, including its films, can directly reflect a democratic consensus'. That view, he suggests, 'ignores the effects of inequalities of power in the economy, politics and culture in determining not only what is shown, but also what is not shown'. Those may mean 'that the ideas to be found in films may be imposed upon their viewers; may be most consistent with the interests of the most powerful; and may simply be misleading, illusory or marginal'.[45]

The same kind of question is raised, perhaps even more forcefully, in respect of TV. In a market-based system, the fundamental determinant of what is shown is the search for markets and profits. The only alternative is some form of public service broadcasting, financed by subscription or license fee, coupled, perhaps, with the risk of political correctness, if not of direct political intervention.

Again, however, the theorists, themselves coming from the highly educated, may be exaggerating the extent to which mass audiences are captured or manipulated. How vulnerable are they? It may rather be argued that they 'engage' with TV actively, 'not taking what they are presented with for granted, often ignoring and sometimes rejecting the messages broadcast. … Television does not, and cannot, construct and impose its meanings; they can only result from the related interventions of viewers.'[46] There are many reasons for watching a soap opera - entertainment, a topic to talk to others

[45] Dominic Strinati, *An Introduction to Studying Popular Culture*, p.133
[46] Ibid., p.181

about, coping with loneliness, escaping, learning[47] - and there are many ways in which it will as a result be received.

Music requires less 'sunk capital' than film, but it was also made tradable by recording. That too had or has its giants, 'labels' like Sony, Polygram, Warner, EMI and BMG. There is surely, however, more scope for the local than in the case of film, though some local artists will be taken up not only by indies but also by major labels, and they may even become celebrities, and indies may become or be semi-indies. 'Majors plunder indies for talent and trends.'[48] They will, as Hyder puts, 'finance and distribute any form of music deemed to be profitable. ... If anti-establishment music sells, it will be sold by the major labels.' In the Britpop phase of the mid-1990s, Sleeper and Salad released their records on the Indolent label. Though seeming independent, it was in fact a subsidiary of BMG.[49]

In his book on J-rap, Condry suggests that commercialisation captures only part of the scene's dynamics. He argues 'that the analytical divide between the power of culture industries on the one hand, and the organic creativity of underground artists and active fans on the other, should not be viewed as oppositional, but rather in terms of their networked interaction. Record companies, artists, fans and media each bring a particular kind of power in developing this cultural world, but the power of each is contingent on the actions of the others.'[50] 'Music is nothing but dialogic', George Lipsitz maintained[51] But how was it that so much originated in the West? And how is it that rap emerging in black New York was taken up in yellow Tokyo? 'Cover' bands brought Western music to colonial and treaty port Asia, the music of the Anglo-Indian bands of the Raj forming an

---

[47] Ibid., pp. 223–5.
[48] Quoted in Rehan Hyder, *Brimful of Asia*, p.46.
[49] Ibid., pp.48, 56n.
[50] Ian Condry, *Hip-hop Japan*, p.19.
[51] Quoted in Rehan Hyder, *Brimful of Asia*, p.40.

important influence on the *fillum* music of today.[52] Later processes included better communications, travel, low-budget films, records, tapes, CDs, and videos, and now electronic media: chats, downloads, file-sharing, MP3s, the 'piracy' of 'intellectual property'.

You can trace the development of Cambodian rap. Started among the diaspora in Long Beach and elsewhere, it was brought to the homeland by Cambodians returning from the United States, France, and Australia. You can trace particular tunes, too. 'You better not come home', sung in English by a German teen band, was picked up by a Taiwanese band, the lyrics changed to Chinese. In Cambodia it was given Khmer lyrics and a pop tune became a rap tune. Earlier French tunes had gone through similar transitions.[53]

Hip-hop and rap have 'become a vehicle for global youth affiliations and a tool for reworking local identity all over the world'.[54] We need more studies of the process before we comment on globalisation, and perhaps venture on theories that might be more satisfyingly explanatory than the discourse of 'hybridity'. At the risk of their hearing, anthropologists and ethnographers are bringing us useful studies of local music scenes that challenge the cruder concepts of globalisation, such as Jennifer Miloto Matsue's *Making Music in Japan's Underground* [NY, London: Routledge, 2009]. Receiving Western music goes back at least to the Meiji restoration, and it covered popular as well as classical genres. In the Second World War, of course, imported musical forms were banned,

---

[52] Brian Shoesmith, 'Preface', in Allen Chun *et al.* (eds.), *Refashioning Pop Music in Asia: Cosmopolitan Flows, Political Tempos, and Aesthetic Industries* (London: RoutledgeCurzon, 2004), p. xv.

[53] Leakthin Chau-Pech Ollier, "Rapping (in) the Homeland: of Gangs, Angka, and the Cambodian Diasporic Identity", in Leakthin Chau-Pech Ollier and Tim Winter (eds.), *Expressions of Cambodia: The Politics of Tradition, Identity and Change* (London: Routledge, 2006), p.114.

[54] Quoted in Roy Shuker, *Understanding Popular Music Culture* p.106.

but importation was renewed in the occupation period and after. In the 1960s 'group sounds' were given English names, but the group did not merely imitate the Beatles. Koku, folk, followed, not to be confused with traditional *minyo*. The 1970s witnessed the advent of idols, *aidoru*, but underground styles also emerged, and in the 1980s hip-hop was appropriated, the artists 'particularly concerned about how to appropriate this foreign form to meet immediate Japanese needs, while maintaining the integrity and authenticity of the genre'.[55]

Burmese pop offers an apparent contrast. Heather MacLachlan's sympathetic study found the musicians 'committed to reproducing the Anglo-American pop music tradition in their own country'. It was not a matter of 'cultural imperialism', on the one hand, nor, on the other, of a lack of creativity. The musicians 'operate according to the Burmese belief that a 'good song' is one that is meaningful to contemporary audiences and demonstrates its meaningfulness by selling well'. James Thiri, one of the 1960s generation, gathered respect because he could do 'something different'.[56] Though MacLachlan does not suggest it, that was possibly because it reacted against Burma's isolation, was even a kind of protest against it.

Much is in the hands of MNCs in the case of film - they could drive the local product from the market, as happened with P. Ramlee's once very popular films in Malaya[57] - much is also in the hands of individuals and small groups in the case of music. That suggests our discussion of globalisation needs to compare the art forms if it is to reflect on or develop theory about localisation or glocalisation. Different art forms have different organisational and capital needs and the nature of audience involvement differs, even if 'watching' is not merely

---

[55] Jennifer Miloto Matsue, *Making Music in Japan's Underground*, p.75.

[56] Heather MacLachlan, *Burma's Popular Music Industry* (Rochester: University of Rochester Press, 2011), pp.179–80, 69.

[57] James Harding and Ahmad Sarji, *P. Ramlee: The Bright Star* (Petaling Jaya: MPH Publishing, 2011), p.194.

a consumer activity. The impact of newer media must also be considered. Indeed some come to live in virtual isolation, geeks, 'islands in space', the Japanese otaku.[58] The development of 'niche' cultures[59] also suggests a paradox: within 'popular' culture - by contrast at least to the idealised 'folk' culture of the past - lonely individuals find their place, and fanatics, too.

Is there a hegemony? The pop can be absorbed into the mainstream. Slank, which produced several best-selling albums in late New Order Indonesia, bridged the underground and the commercial genres.[60] As in other countries, alternative music was taken up by large recording companies because it would sell.[61] And the elite may act as the Western elite had in the case of the waltz. *Dangdut*, which transformed older-style Malay orchestral music by adding a syncopated drum beat, became popular with lower-class urban Indonesians, then in the 1980s with the middle class. It became indeed a national treasure with patronage from the government party, the army, and the ministers, and sold some 35% of the records in Indonesia in the 1990s.[62] ABRI seemed to pre-figure Tony Blair. But mercifully he did not join in, unlike SBY, who sang on his election campaigns and in the finals of the Indonesian version of the idol contest.[63]

Can the state compete with pop or utilise it? Is it a hegemon in pop music? Or in film/TV, where government companies and finance still have a role? It can censor for

---

[58] Ian Condry, *Hip-hop Japan*, pp.114–15.

[59] Ibid., p. 128.

[60] Krishna Sen and Davd T. Hill, 'Global Industry, National Politics: Popular Music in 'New Order' Indonesia', in Allen Chun *et al.* (eds.), *Refashioning Pop Music in Asia: Cosmopolitan Flows, Political Tempos, and Aesthetic Industries,* p.80.

[61] Ibid., p. 82.

[62] Ibid., p. 76

[63] Ariel Heryanto, "Pop Culture and Competing Identities", in Ariel Heryanto (ed.), *Popular Culture in Indonesia: Fluid Identities in Post-Authoritarian Politics* (London: Routledge, 2008), p.5.

moral and political reasons - even the e-media - it can produce cultural objects, it can control education and broadcasting - but can it appropriate? State intervention risks the unintended result of 'killing the cool', in Beng Huat Chua's phrase, and producers may wish to play down historical or national content so as to reach a wider audience.[64] There are some cases of censorship, though banning the saxophone in Thailand would perhaps be lèse-majesté. A rap singer, Joey Boy, had songs banned by the Department of Culture in the Suchinda period, but it had little effect on sales, and 'the association between delinquency and music, central to American popular culture, is rarely made in Thailand'.[65] Sukarno disliked the Beatles among other things British-made. But thirty years later ABRI held pop concerts. The Philippines had its own version of involvement: one of the pirates was appointed to the Videogram Regulatory Board.[66] And it elected a B-movie idol president, though he did not put up a star performance.

Is pop culture in any case transgressive or subversive? Or is it an outlet that in the end—like 'carnival' in the early modern West—preserves the status quo? It has a seeming illicitness. Hardcore in Tokyo, Matsue suggests, 'creates a sense of illicit intimacy, as performers share a passion for a music with a more limited group … than the fan base for J-pop. Performers feel closer to each other because it is an underground genre, and therefore as if they are participating

---

[64] Nissim Otmazgin and Eyal Ben-Ari, "Cultural Industries and the State in East and Southeast Asia", in Nissim Otmazgin and Eyal Ben-Ari (eds.), *Popular Culture and the State in East and Southeast Asia* (Abingdon: Routledge, 2012), pp.19, 22.

[65] Michael Hayes, "Capitalism and Cultural Relativity: The Thai Pop Industry, Capitalism and Western Cultural Values", in Allen Chun *et al.* (eds.), *Refashioning Pop Music in Asia: Cosmopolitan Flows, Political Tempos, and Aesthetic Industries,* pp.23, 27.

[66] John A. Lent, *The Asian Film Industry*, p.162.

in something illicit.'[67] Rap has become a global phenomenon, and its association with the expression of political dissent has made it 'a global language of resistance'. Using the global networks of international capital, as Hyder puts it, it has 'given a voice to local populations the world over'.[68] But it is probably not very transgressive. 'Some differences are permitted, even made commodifiable, as an act of transgression which simultaneously maintains homogeneity', as Hayes puts it. '[Y]oung people [in Bangkok], Hayes was told, once waved their fists at the military or police in protest, but with pop the young were now waving their fists peacefully at pop concerts.'[69]

Craig Lockard's absorbing study of popular musicians in Southeast Asia offers a rather ambiguous answer. 'It is hard', he says, 'to accept the Frankfurt argument that their music should be perceived largely as a mass-mediated, diversionary reinforcer of the power structure that is chiefly neo-colonial in form, shaped mostly by the imperatives of cultural imperialism.' Co-optation and censorship have featured as well as commodification and commercialisation. Yet popular music has been 'a major vehicle of political commentary' and 'sometimes even of criticism and protest'.[70]

In late nineteenth-century England, Vaughan Williams and his colleagues stepped up the collection of folk-songs, fearing that they would be lost. Similar feelings emerge, not only among Westerners, in regard to Asian music. In Thailand 'the circle of teachers and students [of folk music] is shrinking with

---

[67] Jennifer Miloto Matsue, *Making Music in Japan's Underground*, p. 80.

[68] Rehan Hyder, *Brimful of Asia*, p.52.

[69] Michael Hayes, "Capitalism and Cultural Relativity: The Thai Pop Industry, Capitalism and Western Cultural Values", in Allen Chun *et al.* (eds.), *Refashioning Pop Music in Asia: Cosmopolitan Flows, Political Tempos, and Aesthetic Industries,* pp. 25, 29–30.

[70] Craig A. Lockard, *Dance of Life Popular Music and Politics in Southeast Asia* (Honolulu: University of Hawai'i Press, 1998), pp.268, 271.

every generation…. Folk music lacks the socioeconomic strength to compete with the siren songs of extensively promoted pop music.'[71] Might it be driven out of existence by the advent of fusion or preserved only in some museum form or as a tourist attraction? Somewhat paradoxically government intervention in Bali helped to bring about a popular alienation from the performance of traditional gamelan. Its institutionalisation stopped it communicating to the new generation.[72] Some blame the decline of *cai luong*, a famously syncretic form of Vietnamese staged performance, on state manipulation or encouragement, though it was also defenceless against the penetration of video and other such products after *doi moi*.[73]

Much of the literature is on globalisation and seeks to question whether that swamps the local or leaves open opportunities for the local. Is it a matter of 'cultural imperialism', in Herbert Schiller's phrase?[74] The literature does not seem to address process as fully as it might, though it points out that it is not one way.[75] How does black music

---

[71] Quoted in ibid., pp.178–9.

[72] Zachar Laskewicz, 'Popular Music and Interculturality: The Dynamic Presence of Pop Music in Contemporary Balinese Performance', in Allen Chun *et al.* (eds.), *Refashioning Pop Music in Asia: Cosmopolitan Flows, Political Tempos, and Aesthetic Industries*, p.192

[73] Philip Taylor, "Digesting Reform: Opera and Identity in Ho Chi Minh City", in Lisa Drummond and Mandy Thomas (eds.), *Consuming Urban Culture in Contemporary Vietnam* (London: Routledge Curzon, 2003), pp. 140, 149–50.

[74] Quoted in Penelope Coutas, "Fame, Fortune, Fantasi: Indonesian Idol and the New Celebrity", in Ariel Heryanto, (ed.), *Popular Culture in Indonesia: Fluid Identities in Post-Authoritarian Politics*, p.119.

[75] Allen Chun and Ned Rossiter, 'Introduction: Cultural Imaginaries, Musical Communities, Reflexive Practices', in Allen Chun *et al.* (eds.), *Refashioning Pop Music in Asia: Cosmopolitan Flows, Political Tempos, and Aesthetic Industries*, p.7.

become white? There may be answers: pop travels up a society as well as coming down. How does it become yellow or brown? Less has been said, though there have been studies on what happens to it when it does. The media clearly play a role, as do other means by which culture travels. What of diaspora? - are there parallels to the Indians in the UK whom Hyder studies or the Khmers on the West Coast?

Something has been said of the association of pop culture with the 'soft power' a state may exercise in competition with other states.[76] Very little of the literature relates to the regionalisation that is our focus, and that is both an inspiration and a challenge to us. To some extent regionalisation both depends on and maybe competes with the globalisation that is a more established topic. Is it part of a common current, or is it a counter-current, or a swirl in a current? Indian film music - itself influenced by the cover bands of the colonial period - influenced the development of *dangdut*. Are there other perhaps 'Asian' factors? - an affinity, say, between Canto Pop and Japanese music? Or the familial element in soaps?

Could governments agree to promote it? If they could they seem unlikely to succeed, even if they escaped their nationalism or opposed 'Americanisation': their interference is unlikely to popularise, more likely to deter. The issue seems to be in the hands on the one hand of capitalists and on the other of 'the people'. Neither has yet been sufficiently studied.

If we must still stop short of theory, we should concentrate on process. Possibly we need to consider all three processes - up and down societies and among them - when we consider regionalisation. That, too, still seems very much open to investigation.

And maybe we after all need more understanding of globalisation before we can appraise the possibilities of regionalisation. Why has American culture been so much a part of it? The power of the United States? Its role in the

---

[76] For example, by Galia Press-Barnathan, 'Does Popular Culture Matter to International Relations Scholars', in Otmazgin and Ben-Ari (eds.), *Popular Culture and the State in East and Southeast Asia*, pp.29–45.

media corporations? The appeal of the American dream? The *lingua franca* of English, the use of which by Vietnamese rock-singers the authorities grumbled about?[77] The innovativeness of its own society? Could there be a regionalisation led by the largest Asian power? It seems unlikely: the very fact that American popular culture is global is surely part of its attraction.

The historian is *ipso facto* a member of 'high culture', whatever his or her cultural interests. The present one thinks there is an obligation not to sneer at popular culture, nor to patronise it, and is not certain that Frankfort theory or cultural studies neologisms are not in the end, not only elite talk but elitist, though some go in for a kind of *trahison des clercs*, a Tchaikovsky 4th populism, mixing enthusiasm with analysis, hysteria with history. 'Some educators have a bad conscience', as Jacques Charpentreau put it in the 1960s, 'fearing to appear 'square'....' In the last few years, a kind of 'intellectual terrorism seems to have paralysed those who used to call into question the content of the mass media.'[78] But the present author also thinks there is a duty to preserve and enhance high culture in the face of commercialisation and keep it alive by creativity at a time when it seems to have alienated itself from a substantial audience, though it does not seem that this can be done by borrowing from popular culture as it was once done by borrowing from folk. In Asia, as in the West, we inherit what past generations achieved and left for us, and we should cherish and build on that inheritance. Artists created it at the bidding of wealthy patrons, but their wealth came from the peasants of the Esterhazy estates, the taxpayers of the Tang.

Taken from Intra-Regional Popular Cultural Flows *edited by Xin Chen and Nicholas Tarling (New York: Peter Lang, 2018).*

---

[77] Dale A. Olsen, *Popular Music of Vietnam* (London, New York: Routledge, 2008), p.172

[78] Quoted in John Rigby, *Popular Culture in Modern France* (London: Routledge, 1991), p.45.

10. On Accounts and Explanations

If the possibility of change is accepted, it is the historian's task to give an account of it. '[N]o account can recover the past as it was, because the past is not an account; it was a set of events and situations.' Of these the most detailed account can cover 'only a minute fraction', as Lowenthal puts it.[1] Many were not recorded, but those that were are generally so numerous that the historian has to select. The act of selecting is also an active explanation. Even the most straightforward narrative will contain, more or less implied, a framework of understandings about how things happened, and at least in that sense why they happened.

The current inclination to distinguish 'narrative' historians from 'analytical' is misleading. Narrative, John Tosh tells us, can take the reader 'up a blind alley'.[2] The flow of narrative can convey the impression that what came after was caused by what came before. Practically, too, he suggests, narrative 'imposes a drastic simplification on the treatment of cause … It can only keep two or three threads going at once, so that only a few causes or results will be made apparent.' The difficulties are indeed great, and they are conceptual as well as practical. But to keep analysis and narrative apart is no solution. The 'narrative' historian will have some concept of causation, even if the alley is not well signposted. The 'analytical' historian will have failed to fulfil an essential part of the task if offering no sense of continuity or change over time.

In some accounts of the past the explanation is simple: it is a matter of divine intervention. A conviction about God's presence, however, does not necessarily require a simple account: it can coincide with sophisticated kinds of

---

[1] David Lowenthal, *The Past is a Foreign Country* (Cambridge: Cambridge University Press, 1985), p.215.

[2] John Tosh, *The Pursuit of History* (London and New York: Longmans, 1984), p.117.

explanation that may be held to show the working-out of God's purpose. That was indeed how Ranke himself saw history, 'God dwells, lives, and can be known in all history. Every deed attests to Him, every moment preaches his name, but most of all, it seems to me, the connectedness of history in the large. It stands there like a holy hieroglyph ... May we, for our part, decipher this holy hieroglyph! Even so do we serve God.'[3]

Explanation, if explicit, is commonly described in terms of cause. The word, Michael Oakeshott has argued, cannot be used strictly in the vocabulary of historical discourse. 'When it appears there it should be allowed to be ... no more than an expression of the concern of an historical enquiry to seek significant relationships between historical events and to distinguish between those antecedent conditions which are significant for the understanding of the subsequent and those that are not.'[4] Placing events in temporal sequence is not sufficient. 'Time, and the order of occurrences in time, is a clue, but no more', as R.H. Tawney wrote; 'part of the historian's business is to substitute more significant connections for those of chronology.'[5]

A further step is to find regularities among these connections, and thus to establish expectations or suggest hypotheses. 'Historical explanation ... aims at showing that the event in question was not "a matter of chance", but was to be expected in view of certain antecedent or simultaneous conditions.'[6] Some historians write, indeed, in terms of 'laws' or 'models'. They are, perhaps, among those thinkers whom Isaiah Berlin would have characterised as 'hedgehogs', those

[3] Quoted in Peter Novick, *That Noble Dream. The "Objectivity Question" and the American Historical Profession* (Cambridge: Cambridge University Press, 1988), p.27.

[4] Oakeshott, *On History and Other Essays* (Oxford: Blackwell, 1983), p.88.

[5] Quoted in Tosh, *The pursuit of History*, p.117.

[6] Carl G. Hempel, 'The Function of General Laws in History,' in P. Gardiner (ed.), *Theory of History* (Glencoe, Illinois: The Free Press, 1959), pp.348-9.

who desire to know 'one big thing', as distinct from those who are content to know 'many things', the 'foxes'.[7]

That approach was particularly appealing and it seemed important to show that history was 'scientific', in the sense that its discipline was comparable and indeed similar to the 'hard' sciences, and not merely a collection of facts, more or less appealing to the amateur and more or less boring to the student. 'To become a history, facts have to be put together into a pattern that is understandable and credible; and when that has been achieved, the resulting portrait of the past may become useful as well – a font of practical wisdom upon which people may draw when making decisions and taking action.' Pattern recognition, 'this chef d'oeuvre of human intelligence', is, William H. McNeill argues, 'what natural scientists are up to; it is what historians have always done, whether they knew it or not.'[8]

There was a risk, of course, that the laws or models could be obstructive rather than helpful. The foxes might have the best of the argument, but the intelligent mind hankered after the 'single good story' the hedgehog offered.[9] Yet that might diminish the capacity to apprehend change, and bring back the model seen by Machiavelli, that of a world of repetitious change, a world in which things did not change very much, the perception to which indeed Braudel was tempted on one level at least to succumb. Hedgehog and fox are both required. 'The net of scholarship is woven between two poles: that of distinguishing and that of recognising, the perception of what is different and the discovery of what is the same ... scholarship is definitely a duality, not a choice of either the one or the other, but the necessity for both the one and the other.' G. H. van de Kolff pointed to 'the danger of one-sidedness, which sometimes (in the urge towards unity) leads to a blindness to the facts, sometimes

---

[7] *The Hedgehog and the Fox* (London: Weidenfeld, 1953), p.1.

[8] McNeill, *Mythistory and other essays* (Chicago: Chicago University Press, 1986), p. 5

[9] A phrase used in *Time Literary Supplement*, 22 November 1996.

(under the charm of the rich forms manifested by the empirical object) to details devoid of meaning.'[10]

The other risk was that historians mistook what scientists in fact did. Another great French historian proceeded by hypothesis. '[E]very historical research supposes that the inquiry has a direction at the very first step. In the beginning, there must be a guiding spirit. Mere passive observation, even supposing such a thing were possible, has never contributed anything productive to any science.'[11] Science indeed proceeded in the same way. Scientific laws, Karl Popper argued, might better be regarded as best available hypotheses, offering satisfactory, but only temporarily satisfactory, explanations. Both historian and scientist proceed in some measure by the hypothetico-deductive method or by what might crudely be called the 'hunch'. Facts suggest interpretations; interpretations seek facts, but may be destroyed rather than supported by them. The 'paradigm' of T.S. Kuhn is not far off: it solves an outstanding problem in a way that leads to further progress. But in due course the dominant paradigm, losing its explanatory power, may have to be replaced.[12]

Both science and history also, of course, use metaphor. Metaphor is a transaction between contexts, as I.A. Richards put it, or, in Mueller's definition, 'much less the carrying over of a word from one concept to another than the creation or nearer determination of a new concept by means of an old name'.[13] Used in forming a concept or theory, metaphors may come to constitute 'assumptions of an explanatory, descriptive or metaphysical kind'. They serve to

---

[10] van de Kolff, *Indonesian Economics* (The Hague: van Hoeve, 1961), p. 217.

[11] Marc Bloch, *The Historian's Craft*, trans. Peter Putnam (New York: Vintage, 1953), p.65.

[12] *The Structure of Scientific Revolutions* (Chicago: Chicago University Press, 1970), pp.163ff.

[13] Quoted in W.H. Leatherdale, *The Role of Analogy, Model and Metaphor in Science* (Amsterdam: Elsevier, 1974), pp.99, 125.

make things, processes and structure intuitable.[14] So widely accepted may they become that their metaphysical origin may be forgotten and the original affect lost. 'Field', 'force', 'wave', are cases in point. 'In the literal sense of the word, no doubt, natural selection is a false term', Darwin wrote, 'but who ever objected to chemists speaking of the elective affinities of the various elements? … It has been said that I speak of natural selection as an active power or deity; but who objects to an author speaking of the attraction of gravity as ruling the movement of the planets? Everyone knows what is meant and is implied by such metaphysical expressions; and they are almost necessary for brevity.'[15]

It seems that metaphors go through a change in the course of the transactions between contexts. Their initial attraction is partly derived from the old context, and the borrowing adds to the conviction of the new explanation of which they form part. Subsequently they seem sufficient in their new context, and their new meaning is conventionally accepted. The metaphor dies, and the meaning becomes 'literal'. The process may be related to the shifting of 'paradigms' in the Kuhn analysis.

Historians, too, are famous users of metaphor, but there is a difference, and in some ways they are infamous. Science is an orderly system of metaphors, and history rather a disorderly one. They cannot, of course, be avoided if history is to engage in explanation. Some, indeed, are in such common use that, like those scientists have utilised, they are taken literally, since it would be hard to engage in a historical discourse without them. This chapter could hardly begin without using the word 'cause', and there are other metaphors which are difficult to do without and the use of which, though always worthy weighing, may be sufficiently widely accepted to form a means of explanation. 'Origins',

---

[14] Ibid., pp.173, 200.
[15] Quoted in Gerald N. Izenburg, 'Text, Context, and Psychology in Intellectual History', in H. Kozicki (ed.), *Developments in Modern Historiography* (New York: St Martin's, 1993), p.52.

'trend' and 'development' may be among them. What metaphorical power they had maybe lost, yet a meaning is retained. But 'factor', in the eyes of Elton, was 'outside mathematics, and trading stations and Scottish estates ... a meaningless piece of tired jargon.'[16]

Others the historian should use with caution, if at all. Should states, like men (and women) decline (and fall)? Historians resort to botany and zoology, with seeds, roots, growth, waning and flowering. They resort to Darwin, though as Oakeshott says 'evolution' can survive in historical discourse 'only if it is deprived of any exact meaning: as a fumbling, analogical expression for the slow-paced change exhibited in a large-scale historical enquiry, or simply to denote a concern with *la longue durée* in which alleged historical changes are abridged to become examples of general tendencies.'[17] Historians turned to geography, too: if not, like the politician, happy with the winds of change, they may accept its ebb and flow, explore its watersheds, undertake its survey, encompass its turning-points. You may be 'on the eve' of a revolution, as if night must fall. A 'long fuse' is laid for a great war.

Some such phrases might offer the epitomes the title of a book may need, but they use may not be justified by their usefulness. Do they really have explanatory power? Or are they not, rather too often, short cuts that evade the task of explanation? If historians are or have to be less systematic than the scientists, they must not be lazy. Eternal vigilance is the price of satisfactory explanation. That may not exclude the use of analogy or other tropes, without which their writing might be duller. But they can be no more than suggestive or supplementary so far as explanation is concerned.

If the accusation of laziness is unfair, it is because historians have some excuse. A number of agreed paradigms and the number of 'dead' metaphors available to them is so

---

[16] G.R. Elton, *The Practice of History* (Sydney: Sydney University Press, 1967), p.101.

[17] Oakeshott, *On History and Other Essays*, pp.110-11.

much less than the number of available to the scientists in any one phase of scientific advance. Their 'laws', if they exist, are even less enduring, their theories even more tentative, their language more persistently evocative. But the excuse is not a strong one. The very imprecision to which historians are exposed should in fact compel them to an even greater vigilance. If their paradigms and metaphors are so unreliable, they must be used with greater care. Their hypotheses must be tested with even greater vigour. They must all the more attempt to cut down on subjectivity. The hunch must be more than a mere hunch. 'For the facts of history, even those which in historical parlance figure as "hard and fast", are no more than relevancies: facets of past phenomena which happen to relate to the pre-occupations of historical inquirers at the time of their inquiries.'[18]

The tension between the hedgehog and the fox is increased by the very specificity of history. Are your patterns found simply by neglecting some sequence of events all some areas of activity? And, if so, can that be done safely? Even the explanation of a particular event may be too easily undermined. A whole interpretation might be altered, like Butterfield's of the opening of the war in 1914, as a result of finding some one fact that did not fit in: 'total reconstructions are often necessary when a certain fact has proved to be pivotal or requires not merely to be added to the other facts but to be followed out in the displacements it produces amongst the rest'.[19]

Nor, given the uniqueness of historical events, is it easy, even apart from the demands of chronological narration, to draw the elements of an analytical explanation together. Braudel, for example, did not effectively connect the layers in which he viewed change and continuity over time, though resorting to a number of metaphors. 'At the very least', writes Tosh, 'some distinction needs to be made between background causes and direct causes: the former operate

[18] M. Postan, *Fact and Relevance* (Cambridge: Cambridge University Press, 1971), p. 51.

[19] *History and Human Relations* (London: Collins, 1951), p.207.

over the long term and place the event in question on the agenda of history, so to speak; the latter put the outcome into effect, often in a distinctive shape which no one could have foreseen.' He adduces the example of Lawrence Stone's essay on the causes of the English revolution, which considers 'preconditions', 'precipitants' and 'triggers'.[20] The resort to metaphorical categorisation is not entirely happy. But at least it avoids, unless it merely evades, the difficulty in describing some of the causes as more 'important' or 'significant' than others. Assigning causes to lists of the 'paramount' or 'contributing' is a measurement that Barzun and Graff insist that we cannot make.[21] All are needed, and therefore none more or less significant. Their logic may be persuasive. In fact, however, the historian has to ignore it if analysis, let alone pattern-finding, is to proceed.

Stone, as Tosh puts it, is able to show 'the interaction of long-term factors, such as the spread of Puritanism and the Crown's failure to acquire the instruments of autocracy, with the role of individual personalities and fortuitous events'.[22] The role of 'personalities', an essential focus of 'sound' historiography, is again extraordinarily difficult, if not impossible, to appraise. Tolstoy wrote of the dichotomy between 'free will' and 'inevitability': 'History surveys a presentation of man's life in which the union of those two contradictions has already taken place.'[23] Historians have to study both the conditions under which human beings acted as well as their actions and to relate them; but it is hard to pull them apart, let alone the put them together again. Yet again they have to try. And it can be argued that Marx, for example, succeeded. In the *18 Brumaire* he does not ascribe the success of Louis Napoleon to the operation of a covering law, like the class struggle. The 'miracle' is 'no

---

[20] Tosh, *The Pursuit of History*, p.116.
[21] J. Barzun and H. Graff, *The Modern Researcher*, 4th ed (New York: Harcourt Brace, 1985), p.189.
[22] Ibid, p.116.
[23] *War and Peace*, trans. L. and A. Maude (Oxford: Oxford University Press, 2010), III, p.523.

miracle indeed but the natural result of special circumstances created by the struggle of social forces and the purposive actions of a mediocrity who could use these circumstances to his advantage'. It was not 'inevitable', but nor was it 'accidental'.[24]

Historians are indeed likely to conclude that in some cases the role of personalities is more or less important than in others. 'One war may be almost entirely due to the given conditions and hardly at all the consequence of the conduct of the men involved. Another war maybe almost entirely due to that conduct and hardly at all the consequence of given conditions. It is not enough to state that in every case both levels of inquiry exist. It is necessary in each case to discover the relative weight that should be attached to the two levels of causation.'[25]

The challenge the specificity of history presents to particular analysis, let alone to general laws, is also illustrated by the concept of 'counter-factuality' or 'retrodiction'. This Hugh Trevor-Roper advocated in a lecture he gave on leaving his chair at Oxford in 1980. Suppose Churchill had not emerged in 1940, 'a statesman able to unite all parties, and the people, in the will and confidence to continue what could easily have been represented as a pointless struggle'. Suppose Ultra had not been discovered 'at that historic moment'. Suppose Franco had permitted an attack on Gibraltar. Suppose Mussolini had not disrupted Hitler's plans to invade Russia by a surprise invasion of Greece. Any one of these conditions 'might have changed the whole history of the war'. We have, said Trevor-Roper, to leave some room for the imagination. 'History is not merely what happened; it is what happened in the context of what might

---

[24] See M. Kissel, 'Dialectical Rationality in History: A Paradigmatic Approach to Karl Marx's *The Eighteenth Brumaire of Louis Bonaparte*', in Kozicki (ed.), *Developments in Modern Historiography*, pp.97-8

[25] F.H. Hinsley reviewing A.J.P. Taylor's *The Origins of the Second World War*, *Historical Journal*, 4 (1961) p.227.

have happened. Therefore it must incorporate, as a necessary element, the alternatives, the might-have-beens.'[26]

There is in this, as he saw, the risk of barren speculation. Historians may well feel they have enough to do to explain what happened and should not bother themselves to explain what did not happen. Yet, within limits, it may help in the task of analysis, and in the weighing of the various factors, long- and short-term, circumstantial and personal, that, if necessary in the defiance of logic, the historian is perforce engaged. Conjectures are valid, Lester Stevens tells us, if they relate to actual possibilities at the time. 'If they were possible, then the historian may contribute to our understanding by indicating the alternatives which were open at the time. In some circumstances mere luck or chance was the determining factor ... In other cases, however, decisions were made by men, groups, or nations, and for that reason the "if...then." relationship points up what was a possible course of action that was either rejected or overlooked.'[27]

The historian after all is in no position to experiment like the hard scientist. Butterfield might find a fact that did not fit and required him to reconstitute his explanation. Huxley 'always sought the crucial observation or experiment (the destruction of theory by a "nasty common ugly little fact" of his famous aphorism)'. He could experiment, however: the historian cannot. Nor can the historian proceed by stripping away the contingent or removing the variable factors. In that sense his method cannot be 'scientific', in the sense at least as that has been popularly conceived, 'a restricted stereotype about observation, simplification to tease apart controlling variables, crucial experiment, and prediction with repetition as a test. These classic "billiard ball" models of simple physical systems grant no uniqueness to time and object — indeed, they remove any special character as a confusing

---

[26] *Times Literary Supplement*, 25 July 1980.
[27] Quoted in Stephen Vaughn (ed.), *The Vital Past* (Athens, Georgia: University of Georgia Press 1985), p.329.

variable – less repeatability under common conditions can be compromised.'[28]

History has a method, but it has to rely far more on other fields of knowledge are held to rely on self-discipline and self-awareness, on practised skill and judgment, as against formulae or laws. As Gould says, not all science proceeds in the way it is popularly thought to proceed, though the sciences that do not do so risk, despite the achievement of plate tectonics or molecular phylogeny being degraded as 'soft' or 'merely descriptive'. Similarly, he suggests that when students, made familiar with the popular view of science, 'later confront history, where complex events occur but once in detailed glory, they can only conclude that such a subject must be less than science'.[29] It certainly becomes difficult to teach, especially to adolescents who tend to look for certainties. G.M. Trevelyan quoted A.S. Turberville's protest 'against a tendency to present history to children as a body of ascertained truth, instead of being, what it is, a series of accepted judgments', and went on: 'Of course there are difficulties in teaching children in this excellent way, because the unformed minds crave to be told what is true, not merely what is at present surmised. But I agree that we ought always ourselves to remember and within measure lead our scholars to feel that history is a matter of opinions, various and variable, playing on a body of accepted facts that is itself always expanding ...'[30]

Taken from Nicholas Tarling, Historians and Southeast Asian History *(Auckland: New Zealand Asia Institute, University of Auckland, 2000).*

---

[28] Stephen J. Gould, 'Evolution and the Triumph of Homology, or Why History Matters' *American Scientist*, 70 (1986), pp.65, 64.

[29] Ibid., p.64

[30] Quoted in B. Wormald, 'Everybody's History', *The Listener*, 4 October 1962.

Editorial Notes

Born in Buckinghamshire, England, on February 1st, 1931, Nicholas Tarling was one of the leading historians of South East Asia. A graduate of Cambridge University, he took up his first academic position at the University of Queensland in 1957. In 1965, he moved to the University of Auckland, in New Zealand, where he was made Professor of History in 1968, and where he remained until his retirement in-1996. An inspiring teacher, brilliant researcher, and extremely able administrator, Nicholas served as Dean of the Arts Faculty as well as the University's Deputy Vice Chancellor, also holding positions on many University and Government Committees. Nicholas's talents were not restricted to the purely academic and his interests extended well beyond history into music and theatre. An actor and broadcaster, he was involved in many theatrical productions in the University and outside, as well as hosting a successful opera programme on New Zealand radio and was a regular contributor to *Opera Magazine*. He chaired the Symphonia of Auckland and was a Director of Opera New Zealand, He was appointed a Member of the New Zealand Order of Merit in 1996. He died on May 13th, 2017 while swimming at Narrow Neck Beach on Auckland's North Shore.

Nicholas was a key participant in the Interdisciplinary Colloquium, now the W.D. Joske Colloquium, held in Hobart, Tasmania. Nominally a biennial event, and held for the first time in 2002, the colloquium was originally organised under the auspices of the University of Tasmania's School of Philosophy where one of Nicholas's pupils, Jeff Malpas, was professor. All but four of the essays included here (the exceptions being 'On Opera', 'On Time and Place', 'On Popular Culture', and 'On Accounts and Explanations') were written for and presented at the Colloquium. Nicholas was a lively contributor to the Colloquium which brought together participants from a wide range of disciplines including philosophy, history, literature, and the arts, including music and film, as well as law, medicine, and natural science.

This volume was put together by Jeff Malpas and Rupert Wheeler in the first half of 2020 with the aim of drawing together in one volume Nicholas's more philosophically inclined contributions (always informed by his sensibilities as a historian) into a single publication. The essays appear here (some of which existed only in draft form) with a minimum of editorial adjustment and with corrections as were necessary to ensure clarity, accuracy, and completeness.

In preparing this material for publication, the assistance of Dr Nigel Bond, team leader, cultural collections at the University of Auckland library is gratefully acknowledged.

Printed in Great Britain
by Amazon

57718461R00088